GARDEN
ROOMS

OGDEN TANNER

GARDEN ROOMS

Greenhouse, Sunroom
& Solarium Design

Foreword by Hugh Johnson

LINDEN PRESS/SIMON & SCHUSTER

New York 1986

Published by Linden Press / Simon & Schuster
A Division of Simon & Schuster, Inc.
Simon & Schuster Building
Rockefeller Center
1230 Avenue of the Americas
New York, New York 10020

LINDEN PRESS / SIMON & SCHUSTER
and colophon are trademarks of
Simon & Schuster, Inc.

Designed by Bokuniewicz Inc.

Printed and bound by A. Mondadori, Verona, Italy.

Produced by Smallwood & Stewart
6 Alconbury Road, London E5

Library of Congress Cataloging in Publication Data
Tanner, Ogden.
    Garden rooms.
    Includes index.
    1. Garden rooms.   2. Greenhouses.   3. Conservatories

I. Title.
NA8360.T36   1986   728'.9   85-23844

ISBN 0-671-60274-8

First Edition

1 2 3 4 5 6 7 8 9 10

TABLE OF CONTENTS

What the yacht is to the ocean, the greenhouse is to the garden and the world of plants, yet one doesn't need to be a millionaire or even a real gardener to own and enjoy one of these lovely, sun-filled spaces. With both one sets out to battle the forces of nature: to edit the elements for your private pleasure. Greenhouses, conservato-

Foreword

By Hugh Johnson

ries, and sunrooms are calculated to enhance nature's shifting, subtle palette: but instead of the jubilant opal or threatening gray of the ocean, it is the garden where flowers' colors glow against infinite shades of green.

In England we use the term conservatory: we are conserving what used to be termed "greens"—today we say evergreens—against the winter cold. Orange trees were the first favorites, and the buildings built to shelter them, most spectacularly to shelter 1200 of them in the great terraced gardens of Versailles, were called "orangeries".

The French today call a greenhouse a "serre": a place where plants are stored away and locked up tight against the winter. Their alternative of "jardin d'hiver", winter garden, has a much more sympathetic ring— expresses, in fact, exactly what we

want our greenhouses, conservatories, call them what you like, to be: places to enjoy growing plants when outdoors is an uncomfortable place.

Having said that, the choice is still open wide. With skill and daily application you may fill your greenhouse with precious orchids flowering almost every month of the year. With hardly any skill, and in complete relaxation, you can keep a shady corner under glass perpetually fresh and green with ferns and ivies. Somewhere between, with intermittent fervor but perhaps increasing skill, most of us raise a mixed population of more or less forgiving plants, attempting an ecological compromise between conditions pleasant to us and the quite contradictory needs of our plants.

In building my own conservatory—the first significant addition to our old brick house in eastern England since 1699—I had a very specific purpose. Thick-walled and snug as the house is, it had been built to look inward and keep the weather out. And yet, just outside, mellow brick walls encircle a formal garden which is a joy at all seasons. I wanted a place to sit and see the seasons change, to see the leaves fall and the snow settle as well as the buds bursting and flowers thronging the borders.

I was not asking it to be a room in the house, but a room in the garden. I might have to put on a sweater or two on a cold day, but the frost would be shut out—and above all the wind that bites, ruffles, or teases, according to the season.

A simple calculation told me that for every five extra degrees of minimum temperature I insisted on, my fuel bill would be doubled. But I thought of the richness of the plant life that survives all-but-freezing, bringing spring in February around the Mediterranean; if I could walk from my wintry kitchen straight into a Mediterranean day, even a wintry one, I would gain months on the calendar, and a whole new dimension to the range of plants I could grow.

In summer the conservatory is my Japanese teahouse: I sit in the shade with the blinds drawn down. If the meaning of the universe continues to elude me, I learn a great deal about birds and clouds and shadows. But my secret passion is rain: to sit and enjoy it all around without getting wet is a deep private pleasure.

A garden is an expression of the whole person. A conservatory is the same. If the whole of yours is occupied by seed trays I know you. If a jacuzzi takes up every inch you have laid bare your soul.

Hugh Johnson's conservatory at Saling Hall, England.

Introduction

Probably the most popular single item in home building and remodeling today is the so-called garden room, a space that opens up interiors to light and view and brings the many pleasures of gardening indoors. In essence it is a modern version of the old Victorian conservatory, though with sometimes quite un-Victorian overtones. In its contemporary incarnations it is used in all sorts of ways: for sunbathing in the dead of winter; breakfasting among potted palms; soaking in hot tubs; entertaining dinner guests by candlelight under a sky spangled with stars.

There are many good reasons for considering a garden room, and these aren't the only ones. A glass addition, particularly one built of prefabricated, standard components, is often less expensive than other ways of enlarging a house, and surveys have shown that frequently the investment can be regained when the time comes for resale.

But perhaps the most compelling reason for opening up a home with glass is simply that it permits people to enjoy sunlight and plants as a part of their daily lives. Ample natural light not only cheers up the interior but makes it easier and more pleasant to do virtually anything, from cooking to reading or taking a bath. Moreover, plants are good everyday companions, both relaxing to look at and therapeutic to work with, as both psychologists and gardeners can testify. And with the maximum sun and climate control that a well designed garden room makes possible, you can grow a far greater range of plants indoors than normally.

We use the term "garden room" somewhat loosely, in order to embrace a wide variety of indoor spaces that over the years have been given an equally wide, and sometimes confusing, variety of names. Plants have been grown in sheltered, open-air courtyards since the earliest of times, but the first fully enclosed spaces devised for the purpose were the "orangeries" that wealthy patrons of horticulture used for wintering-over the delicate citrus trees and other exotic plants they began importing from tropical climates more than three centuries ago. At first simple sheds with just enough windows to keep the plants alive—glass was very expensive, and came only in small panes—they gradually evolved into larger glazed structures that were variously called "conservatories", "green houses", "glass houses" or simply "stoves", after the massive, coal-burning contraptions used in colder climates to provide the necessary heat. The buildings continued to grow in scale, finding their way from private estates into public arboretums, where the term "winter garden" was often applied. As the cost of glass came down and framing techniques improved, even middle-class Victorians were able to own a garden room: by the turn of the century manufacturers' promises of "greenhouses for the millions" were being largely fulfilled.

Greenhouses are enjoying a similar popular revival today, though some new names, and wrinkles, have been added in the course of time. Voguish in some circles is the old term "conservatory", which, whatever grandeur it may be intended to convey, is still basically a place for protecting and displaying plants that would not survive in winter outdoors. Another is "solarium", derived largely from glassed-in porches used for sunning and applied to some garden rooms where the major attraction is the sun itself. The meaning of "greenhouse" hasn't changed very much: it is still a structure where—unlike a conservatory or solarium—light, temperature, and humidity can be closely regulated for cultivating a larger variety of tender or out-of-season plants. However, we now have many more techniques of climate control, as well as modern names like "solar greenhouses", "sunspaces", and "solarooms" to describe enclosures that make use of the latest gadgetry to trap, store, and distribute sun heat efficiently.

The evolution was inspired by both convenience and cost. The classic greenhouse was a detached, freestanding structure, enclosed by a single layer of glass and located in the open so the plants in it could receive as much sunlight as possible from all sides. While this generally worked well enough for the plants, there were drawbacks: it had to be built as a separate, four-sided unit, at some expense; utility lines for water, heat, and electricity had to be extended out to it from the house; and the owners frequently had to trudge through rain or snow to tend to their chores.

Finally, as a lot of greenhouse owners discovered with the onset of energy shortages, such a structure could consume a great deal of fuel just to keep the plants alive.

While some greenhouses are still built this way, including commercial ones, a majority today are attached to the house, and many make use of double insulating glass. At the same time the notion of using solar energy for free heat has gained wide acceptance; a properly designed garden room can share its warmth with the rest of a home—indeed, can reduce household heating bills by as much as 25 percent to 50 percent. Part of the boom in adding on such structures in recent years has been due to the much-advertised lure of energy-saving tax credits, but, alas, these expired at the end of 1985. Perhaps that is just as well. It has restored the appeal of a garden room to its intrinsic merits, which are certainly strong enough to stand on their own.

The effect of a garden indoors can be created by something as simple as a few shelves with plants in a south-facing window—or it can be as spectacular, and costly, as adding a glass-enclosed wing large enough for an indoor swimming pool surrounded by a jungle of plants. In the pages that follow we examine the myriad possibilities, and how to achieve them in your own home.

Chapter One

DESIGN SURVEY

Sumptuous playthings of the wealthy, orangeries sheltered coveted citrus trees during cold northern winters and were even occasionally used for banquets at which guests could pick their own desserts. The orangery at Barton Seagrave Hall in England, built in the late 18th century, is an elegant example of the precursor to the conservatory.

The classical taste in garden architecture found both utilitarian and artistic expression in Barton Seagrave's orangery. The graceful glass rotunda and French windows admitted sufficient sun to sustain tender plants through the winter; the cast iron columns of the facade anticipated later glasshouses of the Victorian era.

15

Architectural styles as well as plants were soon being enthusiastically imported from abroad, as wealthy amateurs pursued their fantasies of perpetual spring indoors. One of the grandest examples of the newly popular "Indian Style" was Sezincote, a fanciful country mansion in Gloucestershire built in 1806 for a retired nabob who had served the Empire in India.

Sezincote is an Englishman's fantasy of Moorish pleasure; a pasha's seraglio of carved stone, cast iron, and tinted glass, attached to the main house by a gracefully curving gallery. Its gardens were planted with ferns and bamboos to create an Oriental effect.

One of the finest early American conservatories is at Rockwood, a private estate built in 1852 near Wilmington, Delaware. Attached to the east end of a rural Gothic manor house, it provides an enchanting view from the drawing room and the garden.

Slender, graceful cast iron columns decorated with scrolled wood brackets and pendant Gothic arches support the conservatory roof. The creamy yellows and rich violet browns of the interior make a luminous Victorian backdrop for palms, ferns, and other exotic species, with yellow chrysanthemums, pink begonias, and red geraniums adding bright dashes of color. At the far end of the room the vista is brought to a focus by a fountain pool nestled in an alcove hung with a large Boston fern.

Lednice, a neo-Gothic castle in southern Moravia, includes several 19th century tropical glasshouses. Built by the royal family of Liechtenstein as adjuncts to one of their many eastern European homes, the conservatories reflect the popularity of winter gardens throughout Europe.

The early 19th century conservatory at Bicton Gardens, Devon, reflects a technological and aesthetic daring unusual for its day. The fluid forms of the domes are attributed to the English designer J. C. Loudon, who used wrought iron sash bars and overlapping "fish scale" panes of glass to shed rain and provide a seal against heat loss. Bicton's owner and his horticulturist raised pineapples, grapes, and other delicacies within its domes.

The baroque style of Harlaxton Manor inspired William Burn to create a magnificent winter garden in the 1840s. One of the largest attached glasshouses of the period, it is composed of five separate sections on the south side of the house. Embellished with a peaked glass roof, its stone structure and squared glass doors are more akin to the orangeries of the 18th century than to its 19th century peers.

Cool stone floors and decorative iron grilles conceal hot water pipes, while insulating screens and doors permit varying climates for each of the rooms. The centerpiece of the conservatory is a fountain pool planted with waterlilies and other aquatic species.

Two Greek revival statues, echoed by the forms of the cypress trees against the far wall, stand guard at the entrance to the pool room, slightly raised above the level of the house. Now restored to its earlier grandeur, Harlaxton is filled with plantings similar to those of the original owner.

The gentle crescent of Syon House conservatory, built between 1820 and 1827, forms a sheltering semicircle around the private gardens of Syon estate. Set in a landscaped park stretching down to the Thames, the Italianate design of Charles Fowler featured a soaring, cathedral-like dome. While the facade clings to the classical appearance of stone, the 60-foot-high structure displayed the latest construction techniques in iron and glass.

Rising two stories on the south wing of an 1850s addition to a medieval English country house, the conservatory at Flintham Hall is as eccentric as it is daring. Surmounted by a vaulted glass roof, it adjoins a grandly furnished library.

The subdued atmosphere of Flintham's library is tempered by the verdant conservatory, seen through decorated Italianate masonry arches. The greenhouse interior lends an air of comfort and opulence to the somber mansion.

The library balcony affords a sweeping view down into the conservatory, which is large enough to house a full-grown mimosa tree. Statues and fountains are overgrown with honeysuckle, Virginia creeper, and plumbago. Above, baskets display geraniums and exotic ferns.

A wrought iron staircase with palm motif adorns the Palm House of the Royal Botanical Gardens at Kew, a conservatory whose interior height of nearly 70 feet was designed to accommodate the tallest tropical trees. Built in the 1840s, the Palm House was inspired by Queen Victoria's earlier visit to the Duke of Devonshire's celebrated "Great Stove" at Chatsworth, a greenhouse so large her entourage drove down its aisles in horse-drawn carriages, admiring tropical birds that flew among the palms. The Palm House, in turn, inspired an equally famous glass structure: Joseph Paxton's Crystal Palace, built for the Great Exhibition of 1851.

One of several greenhouses at Kew, the Temperate House was begun in 1860. Larger than even the Palm House, it was designed for plants of borderline hardiness.

In summer an elaborate mechanism allowed the roof sections to be stacked upon each other, opening the interior to the breeze. Decimus Burton's design included ornamental piers topped by urns.

A conservatory housing an indoor pool, this recent addition to a Gothic Revival home in England's West Country was built not only for swimming but also to house the owner's eclectic collection of stained and enamelled glass. Architect Martin Johnson's light-filled refuge is in perfect keeping with the Victorian rectory.

Colorful tiles, stained glass, and creeping vines add a jewel-toned light to an adjoining space that serves as dining room, sitting room, and recreation room. Beautifully painted Doulton jardinieres raised on pedestals are used as cachepots for smaller plants.

First used to transport delicate plant species overseas, the glass-sided Wardian case encouraged the Victorian passion for gardening under glass. Soon adopted for use as a miniature conservatory, it became a familiar sight in stylish drawing rooms. This exterior version, at Kensington's Linley Sambourne House, is one of the few remaining examples of its kind.

An open porch on this French house was enclosed in glass to create a garden room available for use year round. The retention of the original stone balustrade and a profusion of lush, vining greenery softens the effect of the modern addition.

Unable to change the facade of three small houses they had joined together, the owners of this Boulogne townhouse chose instead to add on to the back. The top structure was prefabricated, and serves well for plants or people in moderate weather; the custom-built ground floor conservatory, sturdily constructed with insulating glass, is designed for use all year.

U nusable space on a city rooftop was reclaimed with the addition
of a standard Lord & Burnham
greenhouse. Used as a working
plant nursery, it also lends light
and color to adjoining rooms, and
to the bleak winter cityscape.

A cramped 18th century French gatehouse was restored with a greenhouse addition without obscuring its stylistic heritage. While the front of the house presents a formal facade to passers-by, the rear opens to the garden through walls of glass. The owners transformed the greenhouse into a kitchen-dining room, thus enlarging the meager ground-floor living space and flooding the interior with sunlight year round.

The new kitchen conservatory is attached to the interior by double glass doors, which also serve as a summer entrance to the house. The old kitchen was converted into a child's bedroom.

Brilliant azaleas and ethereal dogwoods in this Connecticut garden combine with perennial wildflowers to ensure a constantly changing palette designed for peak bloom in early May. The plantings also help to soften the lines of an aluminum-framed greenhouse, which the owners use to grow seedlings, orchids, and bulbs.

A Victorian porch, its ornamental framework painted a brilliant ultramarine, was enclosed in glass to create a winter garden for modern living in northern France. Two sets of French doors align with interior windows to allow cool breezes to blow through the solarium and into the rooms beyond.

A nearly circular glass structure affords added living space
for this ancient French chateau.
Golden light radiates through the
ruffled ceiling drapes and is re-
flected onto the blond wood of
interior furnishings.

A second home used year round, this Tudor-style house in New York State has north-facing living areas that can be cold and dark in winter. The owners wanted a space filled with warmth, sun, and plants year-round so architect Constantine Vichey designed a prow-shaped conservatory at the end of a south-facing wing.

Set in a grove of linden trees, the conservatory is shaded in summer but sunny in winter. The adjoining wall to the house includes a fireplace so that the room can be enjoyed even on cold winter evenings.

Echoing the distinctive lines of the house, the high arched roof adds a dramatic scale to the room and is tall enough for palm trees. Smaller potted plants are grouped at eye-level and on the brick floor, and moisture-loving plants are positioned around a small stone pool.

A prism-like, triangular atrium of glass opens up a lakeside house in Connecticut designed by architect Warren Arthur. Partly inspired by the restrictions of a narrow lot, it serves as a spacious, welcoming main entrance reached from the road (at left) through a privacy wall and across a broad wooden deck. At the same time it captures desirable east and south light to illuminate a stair well, a lower living room, and a mezzanine dining area; it also extends the views from these spaces down the length of the lake.

Architect Alan Buchsbaum adapted a standard sunroom unit to a Manhattan rooftop to gain needed space. The addition, decorated in bold, eclectic style with some Art Deco pieces, bathes the interior in sun by day and affords a fine view of the lighted Empire State Building at night. Tinted glass was used to reduce sky glare; excessive sun can be controlled by slatted blinds that roll down on tracks inside the glass.

The transparent walls and ceiling of a penthouse provide stunning views of New York City's skyline. The spare lines of the furniture are in keeping with their glass and steel surroundings, while wood floors and a contemporary rug inject much-needed spots of color.

A winter garden and summer sunroom were created when the owner of this Parisian solarium enclosed an outdoor terrace to enlarge his living space. The delicate green plantings and clean lines of the 1930s style white furnishings create a restful and sophisticated environment. Unseen to the right, a more formal living room uses mirrors to reflect sunlight into the rest of the apartment.

Architect and sculptor Harry Stein designed this Manhattan rooftop extension for a pied à terre. An automatic solar shade of transparent fiberglass mesh admits sunlight, cutting 80 percent of the heat, and the top windows and entire living room wall open onto an encircling redwood desk, which doubles the space available for indoor-outdoor living.

This artist's house in the Hollywood hills overlooks canyon scenery through a glass wall. The window faces northwest to capture prevailing breezes; adjoining French glass doors open onto a veranda. The outdoor feeling is enhanced by 1920s wicker seating, a cool pink and sea green color scheme, and a painted rug by Annie Kelly.

A narrow skylight running the length of the room ensures that the studio is filled with an even level of light throughout the day.

A porthole window in the solid back wall frames the sunny conservatory. A circular table can be set beneath it for formal dinner parties, while summery rattan furniture covered with washable white duck adds to the feeling of spaciousness and light.

Recently added to a neo-Georgian home in New York's Westchester County, this glass structure was designed as a pavilion where the owners could entertain guests. Machin Designs, a fabricator of modern conservatories that recall Victorian ones, tailored standard components to a spacious exuberance, using an ogee roof for added distinction. Ceiling fans and an automatic ventilation system maintain comfort in summer; in the winter the space is warmed by hot-air ducts.

The glass breezeway contains a bathroom and bar to serve parties. On warm days the French doors are thrown open to the garden, and at night the stars and moon can be viewed through the glass roof.

An unusual and graceful conservatory, shaped as a shallow-half-oval in both elevation and plan, was attached to the castle-like wall of an English country estate in 1832. Designed by Decimus Burton, the structure attempted to make the most of the changing angle of the sun as it arched through the sky during the day. To avoid overheating, vents are opened to draw in fresh air at the bottom and exhaust warm air at the top.

A modern, two-story addition to a London home was custom made with an imposing semicircular roof, echoing the curvilinear design of the house facade. The structure extends the living areas for displaying plants, dining, and relaxing in the sun.

51

A tiny, crumbling cottage on the Cornwall coast was transformed into an artist's studio and beach home by the addition of a two-story glass wall. The transparent Mondrian grid frames a constantly changing panorama of sea and sky, while adding structural integrity to the building itself. Pristine white walls and high gloss blue floors visually dissolve the boundaries of the house.

Upstairs, the artist's studio-bedroom is flooded with light through a skylight continuation of the glass wall. The glass wall, spare furnishings, and uninterrupted color scheme unify the two levels and create an illusion of spaciousness.

French doors open invitingly to the garden in a sunny room at Iford Manor, near Bradford-on-Avon, part of an 18th century cloistered chapel which became this conservatory. In the early 20th century the garden designer Harold Peto, a devotee of Italian landscaping, designed the garden as a series of planted terraces embellished with sculptures and architectural ornaments.

The seduction of a greenhouse on a summer's afternoon is exemplified by this enchanting English sitting room. Pastel Lloyd Loom chairs, masses of pink geraniums, and the dappled light of an overhead vine create a dreamily romantic setting for reading, eating, or daydreaming.

This city home in New York began as raw industrial space lit by
a large, old-fashioned skylight. The
20-foot-square steel structure was
reglazed with wire glass, an extra
floor was built, and a door was
added for roof access.

Beneath the skylight a new mezzanine floor is used as a bright and spacious living room. In warm weather the lower frosted windows pivot like awnings to ventilate the interior, assisted by an exhaust system and a central ceiling fan. The lower floor is lit by two openings above the dining room and staircase. Blond wood and white walls reflect additional daylight into all corners of the duplex.

A skylight and an Oriental "moon window" illuminate a California breakfast room by architect Brian Alfred Murphy. The window frames a view of an outdoor pool surrounded by banana trees and other tropical plants. The black and white tiles of the pool are echoed on the counter in the foreground, and the garden theme is carried out in whimsical vegetable furniture designed by Lisa Lombardi.

An architect's Parisian duplex suffered from a kitchen that was both small and impractical. A south-facing glass addition on the second floor created a light-filled kitchen and breakfast nook overlooking a garden, and illuminated a stairwell and mezzanine beyond.

The south-facing sun porch in this passive solar home in Massachusetts was designed by Don Metz for informal living and innovative heating. Equipped with a hot tub for lazy soaking, the room is furnished in country-style wicker and floored in quarry tile for easy maintenance and heat retention. Except in the coldest weather, the room's natural warmth is sufficient to heat the whole house.

A dark, traditional home in the Georgetown section of Washington D.C. was remodeled by architect James Ritter and designer Suzanne Shaw, who converted an existing porch into a luxurious garden room spa. The space centers on a large whirlpool bath, with a separate hot tub to one side enclosed by a screen of natural wood. A variety of handsome plantings includes two fig trees in oversize clay pots. Sliding glass doors open onto the garden, while light streams in through overhead windows.

An aura of Edwardian peace is achieved in this glassed-in living pavilion. White woodwork, wicker furniture and terra cotta tile floors create a year-round feeling of summer.

A Dutch architect blended traditional Balinese architecture with modern design ideas to create this soothing pavilion in Bali. The wood-frame thatch roof is an indigenous Balinese design while modern setees and pristine white floors are spiked with brilliantly colored pillows of local fabric. A continuous water pond surrounds the building, and cool breezes blow constantly across the room.

Chapter Two

FORM AND FUNCTION

A kitchen was created out of unused second-floor space by erecting a glass enclosure over a garage roof. Although actual footage is limited, the greenhouse windows lend a feeling of spaciousness. Doors open onto a circular iron staircase to the backyard, simplifying outdoor meals.

The ideal kitchen, to most cooks, would integrate unlimited storage and work space with plenty of natural light. This is as much an aesthetic as a functional preference. It is far easier and more pleasa[n]t[?] cook in a light, airy room, an[d] nuances of the cook's art ar[e] enhanced when the kitchen is [?] in sun. In Mediterranean c[ountries] much of the preparation of [?] done outdoors, and a kit[chen]

Kitchen Sunrooms

room provides the nearest equivalent to this in more northerly locations. Many people like to hold cookouts or parties outside in good weather, and such an area also provides a natural transition from the kitchen proper to the terrace or patio during the warmer months.

As they are generally located on the ground floor, most kitchens are good candidates for a glazed extension, which can incorporate space from a backyard or patio. But kitchens, particularly apartment kitchens, are also good places for adding a modest window greenhouse or skylight, which will not increase the working area but will magnify the sense of space.

As an added bonus, a sunroom makes the luxury of a year-round

A high-tech kitchen and eating area, designed for this modern glass addition, was enlivened with sea foam green walls and contrasting dark wood cabinets. A center island work area maximizes efficiency and minimizes the division between indoors and outdoors.

The kitchen in a 150-year-old house was enlarged and given new life with the addition of a Lord & Burnham greenhouse. Continuous quarry tile flooring unifies this kitchen and breakfast nook with an outdoor patio. For added shade and ventilation, designer Michael Kalil planted three evergreens at the southern corner of the greenhouse and installed thermostatic controls that open the top windows when temperatures climb.

A plant-filled miniature greenhouse attached to this kitchen window lightens a dark interior and obscures an unpleasant view. The counter serves as desk and snack area and is brightened by accessories and plants. Window bumpouts can often be installed without a carpenter or contractor.

kitchen garden attainable. Plants enjoy the higher humidity in a kitchen, and an abundance of natural light multiplies the possibilities of plants that can be grown. Freshly picked mint or basil, tomatoes or lettuce have a flavor that is far superior to store-bought produce. A plentiful supply generally requires the space and controlled climate of a working greenhouse, and it may be feasible to build one right off the kitchen. But even a small window greenhouse will support a wide range of herbs which will lend color and fragrance to the kitchen, and incomparable freshness and flavor to food. A basic garden might include parsley, basil, rosemary, and thyme; pots of lavender or sweet marjoram will add fragrance, and nasturtiums, chives, or scented geraniums will inject color.

One very practical advantage of converting a kitchen into a garden room is that the necessary water supply and workspace are already there. It is a simple matter to fill a watering can to tend nearby plants, to immerse a badly dried-out specimen in the sink, and to perform messy chores like sowing seeds, rooting cuttings, or repotting plants. Because a kitchen is apt to be relatively warm, it is better to choose plants that prefer warm or intermediate temperatures. An adequate ventilation system for the stove should be used during cooking to prevent airborne grease from accumulating on plant leaves, whose pores must be open to breathe.

Materials suitable to kitchens generally lend themselves well to garden rooms. A handsome, hard-wearing floor of ceramic tile, for example, is durable and impervious to moisture. So generally, are slate and paver bricks made specifically for flooring, but it is wise to treat them with a wax or a clear sealer to protect them from spills and stains.

Softer and warmer underfoot, wood is highly versatile but should be treated with a sealer and polyurethane finish. Less costly is the resilient vinyl (tile or vinyl sheet) flooring commonly used in kitchens.

A small artist's studio in New York state was enlarged into year-round living space through the addition of a conservatory. An extension of the kitchen, the space can be completely closed off to save heating costs during the winter when the studio is unoccupied. Used as a working greenhouse and a dining room, its temperature is kept comfortable for people and hardy plants.

$\mathbf{A}$ growing French family added more space to their home with this almost free-standing sunroom. The south-facing addition uses tinted glass for shading and a light aluminum design to relieve a heavy exterior gabled wall. Warm toned oak details and brass sink and light fixtures soften the spare architectural lines.

Enlarging and modernizing a California kitchen, Eric Moss Architects decided that both cabinets and a window were needed at this juncture of the room. German plastic cabinets were installed, and a window punched through the middle. With the addition of an overhead skylight, the unused, dark area became bright, versatile, and amusing.

Being the focal point of most homes, the living room is a natural choice for treatment as a garden room. Large skylights or glass walls will create a new feeling of spaciousness as they introduce outdoor views and the changing moods of natural light. More practically, a sunroom–living area allows the flexibility of an indoor–outdoor lifestyle and perhaps best of all, it brings into

Living Areas

the home a garden which can be enjoyed year-round.

A living area with a sunroom addition is turned into a much more versatile room often serving during good weather much like the old-fashioned porch. In summer, with the doors thrown open to the backyard, it becomes an outdoor room, giving natural access to a pool, bringing a gardener closer to his or her passion, and forming a natural stage for entertaining.

While considering the home's main living space as a garden room, don't neglect the more mundane areas that serve it. Entranceways form our first impressions of a home, but too often they are dark, constricted spaces that are neither as inviting nor as memorable as they can be. A small glazed structure, or even a larger sun-

room added to an entrance, will provide a welcoming introduction to a home and act as an air lock to stop cold winter air from rushing indoors when the front door is opened. Similarly, a hall along an outer wall can be turned into a plant- and and sun-filled gallery when opened up with glass. A simple skylight with plantings beneath it will transform even a dreary interior hall into a pocket-sized atrium of sunlight and foliage.

A modern solarium in an English city home is furnished with austere simplicity, relying for its embellishment on the richly planted garden outside. The outdoor feeling is echoed by a palm placed in the corner, and the potted plants on a table of Nile green.

Black and white tile flooring, white wicker furniture, diffused light and summery flowers make this French solarium reminiscent of a calmer age. The garden is extended inside by means of a partial earthen floor as if a glass curtain had dropped to capture growing plants indoors.

A simple glass enclosure serves as a protected sitting area for a modern vacation home in the south of France. While not a fully insulated greenhouse, the sheltered sitting area extends the season for outdoor reading and sunbathing.

An appealing clutter and eccentricity mark this Edwardian solarium in 17th century Clonegal castle in Ireland which is used as a reading room. Vines trained beneath the glass ceiling and abstract patterned tile floor lend a Mediterranean feeling.

Charles Jencks transformed his 1840s Georgian terraced house by employing a symbolic vocabulary of motifs, including playful references to recurrent themes—the universe, the seasons, and natural life Large plate-glass windows blur the division between indoors and out, offering varying perspectives on the seasons. A curving double staircase links the main floor to the garden below.

The south-facing Sundial Room contains, appropriately, a large solar window overlooking the garden. Jencks plans to further minimize the boundary between house and garden with extensive indoor plants and a succession of seasonal plantings outdoors that come into bloom in a sundial pattern.

S un bathes the amber colors of the Summer Room in lambent light. The architect-designed table and chairs were inspired by elements of the solar system, while ceiling beams echo Apollo's arrows of the sun.

This charming greenhouse is a sunny and cheerful family room, with space for a billiard table, daybed, chairs, and a breakfast table. French doors to the house can be closed to control temperature and reduce noise, while outside doors lead directly to the garden.

This flower-filled English conservatory forms an insulating and welcoming addition to the back porch, and is visible from the breakfast room bay window. A tranquil spot to read or garden, the masses of geraniums and foliage plants against the glass wall offer semi-privacy from the backyard.

An unremarkable entranceway became a dramatic foil for this London home when enclosed by glass. The pitched roof is a subtle reference to the architecture of the house and lends a more inviting touch to the modern design. Warmed by the sun, the glass portico also serves as an air lock to stop cold winds from entering the house.

Flowering plants and wicker furniture transform this small Edwardian conservatory into a romantic dining room. Stained glass and terra cotta flooring enhance the intimate effect.

A pleasurable meal is founded on good food, but its full enjoyment depends on its setting. For most of us, an eating area should be as varied as the meals we eat and as versatile as the occasions when we serve food, functioning equally well for a family breakfast as for a formal dinner party. Setting a dining area in a garden room is an effective way of capturing these daily rhythms, as it reflects the cycles of the day and seasons.

Dining Rooms

Set with a small table and chairs, even a tiny garden room can be filled with plants, providing a sunny retreat in winter. A larger glass addition can be an informal family eating area near the kitchen. But more formal dining areas are often designed with their view, as much as solar benefits, in mind. Since garden rooms visually bring the outdoors in, they are the ideal way to exploit a dramatic view or a beautiful garden, providing a continually changing setting for dining. At night, carefully planned outdoor lighting will preserve and possibly heighten the drama of the setting.

Porch and garden furniture designed for outdoor use is especially suitable for a casual dining area; and wicker, cane, rattan, or wrought iron tables and chairs will echo the garden theme. The design and decoration of more formal dining areas can follow any taste, bearing in mind that fabrics, wallpapers, and carpeting exposed to sun should be fade-resistant. Ventilation and shading are as important in dining rooms as in any other living area, as much to diminish excessive heat as to temper uncomfortably bright sun during meals.

The entire side of a New Jersey house was glassed in to create an airy two-story dining room. Grey tile floors unify the space and absorb heat for release at night, while flowering plants bloom year-round on the sun-flooded cabinets. A balcony was built beneath second-story windows, and French doors below close off the solarium when necessary. White cloth blinds operated by a pulley system shade people and plants from the midday sun.

The dining room in this Vermont country house includes a small greenhouse addition. A shading vine and seasonal plants flourish inside, casting dappled light on the dining table.

This sunroom was installed as a glassed-in dining room. The blond wood floor and white painted window frames create an airy, summery feeling while the combination of formal and informal furnishings unify house and garden. In warm weather doors can be opened onto the backyard to admit breezes.

A city house and garden were linked by this versatile summer dining area. On fine days it can be opened completely; on rainy days the folding doors can be closed to insulate the diners.

This semi circular\solarium was built to increase space in an old French house without affecting the facade. It has been kept low and wide so as not to obscure second-story windows and the lawn was sloped up to create a clear view when seated indoors. Blue tinted glass and bright green struts relate the contemporary structure to the outdoors.

Almost any garden room or glass addition—even a skylight—will add some warmth to a house during periods when it is exposed to the sun, but it will also lose that warmth, and more, on cloudy days and cold winter nights unless it is designed to be solar–efficient. The most effective solar collector is a relatively long, narrow glass structure, facing as near south as possible to

Solar Sunrooms

catch a maximum of the sun's rays during the day in winter—when the house needs this heat the most. But just as importantly, the space should be designed so that it can be closed off at night when its temperature falls, so that it won't drain heat away from the rest of the house.

The most economical way to insulate the area is to leave the exterior wall intact so that existing windows and doors can be opened and closed to regulate the exchange of heat between the two areas. Equally, some form of insulation for the glass, such as heavy blinds, will reduce the fall in temperature at night.

Even a narrow solar space will collect heat efficiently. Manufacturers sell units as shallow as 3 feet, which are, in effect, large bay windows. But to get some use out of the space besides heat collection, it should be at least 6 to 8 feet wide.

Still, the key to any passive solar heating system is incorporating what engineers call thermal mass in the design: materials that absorb the sun's warmth when it strikes them during the day, then store the warmth for gradual release at night. The most common material with thermal mass is masonry—a floor of brick, of crushed stone, or of ceramic tile laid on a concrete slab; a back wall of brick, concrete block or stone (the thicker the mass of masonry, the more sun heat it will store). Even more efficient is water, contained in clear plastic cylinders or black-painted drums, as explained in Chapter 5.

Once the sun's heat has been collected, openings high on the exterior wall of the house where rising warm air accumulates will allow it to flow naturally indoors. Return openings low on the wall will allow cooler air to flow from the house into the outer space to be warmed in turn, thereby setting up a natural convection cycle.

A thermostatically controlled fan in one of the upper vents will make the transfer of heat more efficient; if the fan is reversible, warm air from the house can be forced into the outer space to keep its temperature up at night or on cool days.

Exterior-type sliding glass doors that extend from floor to ceiling can play much the same role as wall vents. When the doors are open during the day, warm air will flow into the house through the upper part of the open-

ings, and cool air will flow out from the house into the sunroom along the floor; when the doors are closed at night, their double glazing will provide insulation from the lower temperatures of the outer space. Sliding glass doors have other merits: they make an outer garden room a visual adjunct to the house, increase the amount of sunlight reaching the interior, and when open are a standing invitation to tend plants or just sit in the sun.

Modern cousins of the old-fashioned open porch, sunrooms can be added to take advantage of views as well as solar benefits. The owners of this house made the most of their outlook on the Connecticut River with a solarium and adjoining deck. Because the river view was to the northeast, architect T. Whitcomb Iglehart faced the room in that direction, but also wrapped it around the corner to capture desirable south sun. The corner section is enclosed as a separate kitchen garden, while the main area, which opens to the living room, is used as a playroom and dining room. Red tile floors retain daytime sun heat, releasing it to help warm the space at night.

It may seem odd to consider a sunroom or skylight addition for a room which we normally use only at night. But waking up to a room flooded with sunlight is one of the most pleasant ways to meet a new day. Masses of plants, moreover, will contribute a softness and serenity to almost any scheme. The addition of a simple bay window, perhaps with a glass roof, will add a new sitting area

Bedrooms

and natural light for plants, which can be set into interior window boxes, hung from the ceiling, or placed on the floor. In winter, the increased moisture transpired by the plants into the air will make the room more comfortable for sleeping.

Not only the master bedroom can benefit from a little remodelling. A dark guest bedroom, normally a fairly cramped space, can be transformed into an airy, light room simply by adding a small skylight or two. If, as is often the case, the bedroom is constricted by a slope of the roof, the height of the room can be pushed out with a stock dormer unit. Taking in generous outdoor views will increase the impression of space and this solution can also be applied to attic conversions.

A central skylight gives a bedroom a spacious outdoor feeling. The owners took advantage of the sunlit area and planted a small indoor garden. A low day bed, Oriental prayer rug, scrolled columns, and potted tropical plants create a Middle-Eastern feeling in the room.

A standard sunroom extension increases light and a sense of space in this second floor bedroom without destroying privacy.

A renovated split-level suburban house incorporates a greenhouse to shelter a below-ground garden area and brighten a dark basement. The minimalist decoration is relieved by the splash of light and color it introduces, while the greenhouse continues the interior design with its natural concrete floor and undisguised structural elements.

A line of vertical windows, shaded by climbing vines, provides both light and privacy in this contemporary French bathroom. Swivel mirrors, at once practical and pleasing, reflect the outside greenery.

The bathroom has undergone a startling transformation over the last decade or two: while the size of the average home has been shrinking, the bathroom has expanded, both in number and size. Once treated as little more than an over-size closet, the bath has become a bright, spacious room in its own right, designed for comfort as much as function. As people have come to

Bathrooms

recognize the restful and therapeutic aspects of bathing, the design and purpose of the bathroom has moved toward that of a retreat or spa. The hot tub has introduced the pleasures of outdoor bathing, and a bathroom in a garden room, or one with generous skylights or sliding glass doors that open onto a garden, can be a truly relaxing place.

A small, dark bathroom is an especially good candidate for remodelling with glass, or for enlarging with a glazed extension. Since many people use the bathroom for dressing and grooming, the added light makes the room more practical as well as more pleasing. An expanded bathroom area can be large enough to contain exercise equipment such as a stationary bicycle, weight-lifting apparatus, or a rowing machine.

Privacy in a garden bathroom can be maintained even with a full glass wall, using conventional curtains or blinds or better still, a screen of plants. Frosted glass or glass block, both of which admit plenty of daylight, can block direct sightlines, and Japanese shoji screens, drawn across the glass when the bathroom is in use, will create a serene and luminous light.

As with kitchen garden rooms, bathrooms have readily available water for plants. They also need similarly water-resistant wall coverings and non-skid floors.

The luxury of an outdoor bath, and the privacy and comfort of an indoor one, are achieved in this glass-roofed bathroom. Glass doors open onto a deck shaded by a pergola, and plants and vibrant green tile unify the two spaces.

In favorable climates a hot tub belongs outdoors since sunshine and scenery are as much a part of its relaxing qualities as its warm

Hot Tubs and Spas

swirling waters. But in cooler climates, an ideal alternative to a natural setting is a garden room, one that can be opened up to a garden or backyard many days of the year.

Like the wood wine vats that inspired them, hot tubs are usually made of durable redwood or cedar staves bound with strong metal hoops. Typically 4 feet deep and 5 or 6 feet across (although they can be 12 feet across or more) hot tubs come with built-in benches for sitting, and optional adjustable jets that create a swirling, massaging effect. Spas, which have jets built in, are of much the same dimensions. Most are made of fiberglass with a tough acrylic lining, which is easier to maintain, and they are available in a greater variety of colors and shapes.

A major consideration in the location of a tub is its weight: most residential floors are designed to support around 40 pounds per square foot, but even a small hot tub when full can exert a pressure of well over 200 pounds. It may be that an existing floor of reinforced concrete is adequate to carry this load, but other floors will almost certainly have to be strengthened in consultation with the manufacturer or a professional engineer.

Spa and hot tub water is generally kept around 100 degrees for its therapeutic effect, and space should be allowed in the design of the room for a separate water heater. To dispel heat and moisture the hot water gives off, the room should have adequate ventilation, probably supplemented with an exhaust fan. Insulating glass will cut down on the condensation as well as heat loss. A tub designed for outdoor use often has a removable protective cover, and this should be left on indoors when the tub or spa is not in use, to reduce evaporation and help maintain the water temperature.

Walls and ceilings adjoining the house should be insulated with a vapor barrier to prevent moisture from penetrating. Finally, all materials and fixtures in the room should be water- and rust-resistant; flooring should be non-skid and sloped toward a drain to carry water away. A good choice underfoot is unglazed ceramic tile or wood decking.

This passive solar greenhouse contributes to the house heating system and at the same time serves as a year-round sun-filled spa. An integral part of the home, it can be entered from both the master bedroom and the living room.

This indoor-outdoor whirlpool bath designed by architect Charles Jencks is tiled in shades of green to form a continuity between the garden and bathroom. Decorations on the tub depict an inverted cosmos loosely based on Baroque domes; above the four seasons are painted on glass lights.

Careful design can often serve to create continuity between different elements. Flowing blue tiling visually merges a hot tub with the adjoining swimming pool; numerous potted plants meld the surrounding area with the outdoors.

Perhaps the ultimate luxury in garden rooms is one that encloses a swimming pool for enjoyment year-round. Depending on budget and taste, the pool can be as small as a "dunk-and-paddle" design for relaxing dips; a larger, narrow lap pool for serious daily exercise; or a standard, outdoor-sized pool with

Indoor Pools

generous space around for plants, tables, and chairs.

Although smaller prefabricated tanks can be built above ground—a necessity if the land behind the house dips sharply away—most pools are solidly embedded in the earth, and for good reason: a 12- by 24-foot pool 6 feet deep contains nearly 13,000 gallons of water and weighs about 54 tons. Most pools are made of reinforced concrete, though metal and fiberglass shells are also used. Concrete is stable, strong, and can adapt to a variety of shapes; fiberglass requires little maintenance and no surface finishing, as its color is integral to the shell.

A climb-out area and walkway around a pool should be at least 3 feet wide around the sides, with a broader deck at one end for sunbathing or entertaining.

Landscape designer Roger Wohrle chose a naturalistic setting for his freeform swimming pool by installing it in his exuberantly planted tropical greenhouse. Masses of orchids, bromeliads, and ferns flourish in the humidity. In keeping with the jungle setting the irregular pool has a black painted bottom, giving it an illusion of added depth.

A contemporary lap pool in Connecticut designed by architect Robert Faesy is sheltered by a passive solar structure with a slanting glass wall facing south. Around the pool, textured quarry tiles are used for non-slip footing; alcoves provide built-in seating and places for displaying plants. A motorized pool cover unrolls from the far end to reduce evaporation and heat loss from the large water surface when the pool is not in use.

Enclosed by a freestanding wood and glass pavilion, an outdoor pool was converted for year-round use. A sauna, spa, and poolside seating area were incorporated into the pavilion, which on sunny days is dappled in aqueous light.

Sun warmth alone cannot be relied upon to maintain the water temperature at the 70 to 75 degrees most people prefer; and provision will have to be made for a heating and filtration system, either under the deck or in a closet to one side, to keep the water pure and comfortable enough for swimming.

Major manufacturers offer greenhouse or sunroom units of various sizes that are adaptable for an indoor pool, or an enclosure can be custom designed. A large body of heated water releases a good deal of moisture to the air, which can result in a steamy atmosphere and heavy condensation on the glass, so it is important to have ample ventilation and insulating glass in colder climates. A row of operable vents along the roof line and sliding glass doors on the sides will accomplish this in winter; in summer the doors can be left completely open to an adjoining terrace or deck to give the effect of an outdoor pool, yet one that is still sheltered enough to be used on chilly, rainy, or windy days.

As with any outdoor pool, the water must be kept in proper balance with chemicals to destroy bacteria and algae. Chlorine and other disinfectants can damage plants around the pool, particularly if splashed water remains on their leaves, so it is prudent to arrange plants in containers or raised beds set a few feet back from the edge. Species that prefer high humidity—bromeliads, many orchids, staghorn ferns, and other tropical plants—will flourish in the moist atmosphere, as long as there is adequate ventilation, but it is desirable to avoid fuchsias, begonias, camellias, and other plants susceptible to mildew and rot.

The traditional lines of this 16th century cottage in Surrey have been extended into a high-tech pool room and spa with a two-story pyramid glass house. Duane-Paul designed the spacious angular addition to accommodate an indoor garden, swimming pool, hot tub, sauna, and guest room.

Inside, the steel and glass structure is softened by abundant potted plants. The overhanging balcony has garden-style seating, and is attached to second floor living areas by a gallery walkway.

The original purpose of greenhouses was to grow plants, and that use is still as prevalent and enjoyable today as it was in the 19th century. A greenhouse can be small or large, although a minimum size to grow a good range of plants is about 12 feet long and 8 feet wide. Like most sunrooms, the longer dimension is usually placed against the house wall in an economical lean-to de-

Working Greenhouses

sign. This layout saves on construction costs and permits the greenhouse to share its sun-generated heat with the house.

Though somewhat less economical in terms of construction and heating, a freestanding unit benefits growing plants by providing them with a more even distribution of light from all sides. It may also be the only solution where space, or exposure to south sun, is limited by the configuration of the house. Freestanding, two-sided units are often attached by their narrow ends to a house and entered through an existing or newly cut door.

In either case, the greenhouse should be placed where it will receive the greatest amount of unobstructed winter sun. The sun's rays are at a lower angle in winter than in summer, and so house eaves, trees,

This Vermont house was designed around two south-facing solar greenhouses, one containing a hot tub, the other a working greenhouse used as a nursery for the extensive outdoor gardens and for houseplants. Both greenhouses are vented to all three floors of the house, and are the major heat source.

Surrounded by a profusion of plantings— shrub roses, cornflowers, ferns, and morning glories— this small working greenhouse is nestled in the far corner of an English garden. But beneath its charm there is a functional purpose. It is set partially below ground for insulation, while its steeply sloping roof maximizes the sunlight admitted for growing plants.

This moderate-size greenhouse uses a knee-wall and lean-to design to reduce heat loss. Positioning the greenhouse slightly below ground level hid much of the unattractive concrete foundation. Landscaping with flowering trees and shrubs softens the shape of the structure and provides shading during the summer.

or other possible obstructions to winter sun must be taken into account. The greenhouse should also be designed so that it can be completely closed off from the rest of the house in order to maintain optimum conditions of temperature and humidity.

The interior need not be elaborate, just workable, as this is a private greenhouse which must satisfy only the gardener. Specimens for display can be brought into the house when desired. Plant benches are normally arranged on the perimeter, with additional island benches in the center if space allows. Greenhouse suppliers stock standard benches, or simple benches can be made out of 1- by 4- or 1- by 6-inch boards supported on a framework of 2- by 4s. They should be a convenient working height and no wider than a comfortable reach, generally 2 to 3 feet if they are accessible only from one side. Aisles between the benches should also be 2 to 3 feet wide.

If the greenhouse is to function as anything more than just a place to shelter sensitive plants during winter, it will need to have running water and electricity. A small sink and potting area installed at one end of a bench near the house, with storage space for pots, soil mixes, and tools will serve as a handy work center. Electrical conduits are necessary for lighting, fans, plant-growing lights, space heaters, humidifiers.

To maximize the space, (in precious short supply in most green-

A window greenhouse is an inexpensive way to increase light and growing space in a house or apartment. Prefabricated units are generally about 1½ feet deep, come in heights and widths to fit most standard-sized windows, and are relatively easy to install. Standard features include double glazing for insulation, top vent panels with insect screens, and one or two shelves. Additional shelves, heaters, thermostats, and fans are available as options in some units.

The owners of this American Victorian house needed a nursery to start seedlings for their summer garden. They erected a Janco double-glazed greenhouse, which has a stone floor for heat retention. A wood hot tub sits on a platform near the kitchen entrance, while picture windows in the family room overlook the sunny greenhouse.

houses), potted plants can be hung from the overhead structure, or set on shelves that are either suspended from the ceiling or arranged in stepped tiers along the walls.

Unlike the floor of a live-in sunroom, that of a working greenhouse should be porous and well-drained so it can be washed down. The ground can even be left completely uncovered, with only flat paving blocks or flagstones laid in the aisles and walkways. A common and highly functional floor is simply a 4-inch layer of coarse gravel or, preferably, angular crushed stone, which more readily stays in place underfoot. A stone or gravel floor will quickly absorb water and dirt, and can be hosed down occasionally to raise humidity for the plants; having some thermal mass, stone, or gravel will also absorb and store sun heat which will be beneficial on chilly winter nights. A still neater floor with much the same attributes is one of bricks loosely laid on sand over the entire area or only in the aisles, with coarse gravel under the benches where it will drain off water and dirt spills from the plants above.

While humidity is desirable in a working greenhouse, it may cause moisture damage to an adjoining house wall made of wood, so it is a good idea to install a vapor barrier between them, or to keep the siding water-resistant with a clear sealer, sealing stain, or paint.

Chapter Three

GARDENING UNDER GLASS

For most people the greatest appeal of a garden room is the simple, and quite marvelous, fact that it can bring a real garden inside a home— one that flourishes winter and summer, affording colorful fresh flowers, fragrant herbs, vegetables, and fruits. Hot tubs and lower heating bills aside, there is nothing quite as luxurious or as satisfying as sitting in a fragrant garden room in midwinter or having a living, continuously changing display of plants year round.

Gardening Under Glass

In the controlled conditions of a conservatory or greenhouse, plants will not merely exist but actually thrive— often putting on a better show than they would in a summer garden outdoors. Almost any kind of garden room, even a small window "bump out " greatly increases the number of species that can be grown successfully indoors. Plantings need not be restricted to old familiar standbys like philodendrons, Swedish ivy, or spider plants; a far wider range of exotic tropical and flowering species can be grown, and without a great deal of time or effort. Many orchids, for example, do not require the steamy jungle conditions some people believe they do. Varieties of cattleyas, cymbidiums, and dendrobiums will flourish when temperatures are on the intermediate to cool side. These and other flowering plants need ample sunlight to blossom, while for shadier areas of a garden room there are many foliage plants that prefer bright indirect light or partial shade.

But besides considering the needs of different plants, it is the arrangement of their various sizes, shapes, and colors that is the key to a successful garden indoors as well as out. Poor planning is one of the most common reasons why a garden room fails to be inviting or interesting. Just as an attractive living room is more than a random collection of furniture, an attractive garden room should be more than an off-hand assortment of plants; there can be few more unhappy sights than an ill-assorted display of struggling plants.

Fortunately, the range of species that will thrive in a garden room is almost limitless. In its protected environment, a gardener is free to indulge a passion for certain favorites, or to devise a planting scheme that might not be practical outdoors. But for the most part, the principles of garden planning are the same. Any good scheme generally has a main, and sometimes a secondary, focal point. In a garden room this can be a

Orchids—which come in thousands of bewitching species and varieties, with flowers ranging from near microscopic dimensions to the size of dinner plates—have been considered the quintessential greenhouse plants since Victorian days. This spectacular display, in a greenhouse at Longwood Gardens near Philadelphia, suggests the spectrum of orchids that can be grown in even a modest garden room.

A veritable jungle of plants in a conservatory of Gothic design shows that a garden room can be planted to be equally as lush as a summer garden outdoors.

single, arresting "architectural" plant like a large flowering shrub or palm; or a grouping of plants of varying heights chosen for a pleasing combination of foliage or flower colors, textures, and forms; or a small indoor fountain or pool, set off by moisture-loving orchids or ferns. If the room is used for dining or entertaining, on the other hand, these activities themselves might more properly be the focal point, with flowers and foliage chosen as a pleasant but unobtrusive backdrop.

Most plants will benefit from careful grouping, even if it is simply placing taller ones at the rear, perhaps on the floor, and positioning smaller plants toward the front, arranged on tables or ledges. Consider color as well. Ferns and palms, and many other plants, contribute foliage but can easily become oppressive in mass—an effect that can be alleviated by introducing some spots of vivid color with one or two flowering plants. Ferns and orchids require similar conditions and a lacy bank of ferns is an ideal backdrop for the orchids' shapes and vivid colors.

Don't confine the plantings to eye level and below. Further interest and an added sense of height is created by foliage and flowers cascading from hanging baskets, and by sun-loving vines, trained against the glass on trellises or wires, to provide pleasing patterns of light and shade (vines, baskets and taller standing plants can also help soften the structural framework of greenhouses, which sometimes tend to have an industrial look).

Most people grow indoor plants in individual containers, to make them easier to move around for different effects, to locate them in the conditions of light and warmth that suit them, and to tend them according to their individual needs. Plants in containers can also be moved outdoors in summer to liven up a terrace or patio, and to escape the extreme conditions of a garden room in midsummer.

Many gardeners, however, like to arrange at least some of their plants in beds to create the effect of an outdoor garden. The simplest way to do this is to group a dozen or more potted plants close together, concealing the tops of their pots with a mulch of bark chips or sphagnum moss and the fronts with a border of loosely set bricks or stones. Unpotted plants can be planted in a raised bed of soil. For proper drainage, the foundations of the bed should be of coarse gravel or crushed rock in contact with the ground below, or of bricks loosely laid on sand so that water drains away. Some gardeners leave sections

This lovely English glasshouse embodies the age-old controls of greenhouse design. The curved glass shape—made of distinctive overlapping panes that resemble fish scales—admits maximum natural light for the plants. Push-out windows allow cross ventilation and prevent overheating.

Foliage and flowering species can be combined for striking contrast. In this conservatory a large, silver-leaved artemisia, and a graceful fan palm behind it, are framed by tall eucalyptus and flowering hibiscus. Colorful accents are provided by fuchsias, geraniums, marigolds, and other smaller potted plants.

of their greenhouse floors open to the soil in order to grow indoor trees or other large-rooted plants.

Garden rooms and greenhouses are commonly divided into categories according to their temperature ranges, with the cooler night highs and lows being most critical. A "cool" room, the most economical in northern climates, is generally one in which the temperature may reach the 50s and 60s (Farenheit) during the day but drops to 45 or 50 degrees on winter nights. An "intermediate" room has winter day temperatures of 60 to 70 degrees and night temperatures of 50 to 60 degrees. In a "warm" room, day temperatures are around 65 to 75 degrees, and night temperatures are kept between 60 and 70 degrees.

For most plants, a cool or intermediate garden room is adequate. In such a room people and plants can coexist comfortably during the day, while the temperature can be allowed to drop at night when the room is not in use, giving the plants the coolness they prefer. If necessary, sliding doors made of double glass can insulate the rest of the house from the garden room at night.

A few favorite heat-loving species may be marginal under cool or intermediate conditions, but warmth for these plants can be provided individually on especially cold nights by a portable electric heater, or by using electric heating coils in the plant beds. These coils, sold by many greenhouse and plant suppliers, provide root warmth only for plants that need it, rather than heating the en-

tire room. Expert indoor gardeners have found that "bottom" or "bench" heating of 60 to 70 degrees can actually make plants healthier and sturdier, with better root growth, and at the same time allow air temperatures to be maintained at an economical 50 degrees or less. The coils can also be used to start new plants: bottom heat increases the percentage of seeds that will germinate in a seed bed and helps cuttings take root in half the usual time.

Most plants, with the exception of dry-region natives like cacti, need a certain amount of moisture in the air, generally a relative humidity of 40 to 50 percent; some species native to moist climates prefer 60 percent or more. Such levels of humidity are comfortable for humans but are much easier to maintain when the air is cool.

In many homes, however, winter heating and closed windows reduce the humidity levels to 25 percent or less, and the high temperatures that some people like to maintain further parch the air, sometimes to a bone-dry 10 percent. A humidifying unit attached to a central warm-air system or an inexpensive cool-vapor room humidifier can raise the humidity to a level more comfortable for people and plants.

A simpler, and often adequate, method of maintaining good humidity is to group plants together so each will benefit from the moisture transpired by the others' leaves (but allow some space for air to circulate to discourage fungus and other diseases).

Banked masses of bright color can also be as effective in a garden room as they are in the open air. At left, close-set pots of annuals—in this case, butterfly flowers (*Schizanthus*) in harmonious whites, pinks, and purples—give the appearance of a garden border. In the background, orange-flowered flame vines and red ivy geraniums form a vivid curtain of flowers against a white wall.

A fern garden creates quite the opposite effect of planting for color. Here the design is guided by the various patterns and textures of foliage, which combine to produce a soothing evergreen environment.

To increase the humidity further, place individual or grouped plants on shallow saucers or trays filled with an inch or so of gravel or decorative pebbles. Keep the saucers or trays filled with water to just below the surface of the pebbles (don't let pots with holes in their bottoms actually stand in the water, which will keep the soil soggy and encourage rotting of the roots). Humidity around individual plants can also be raised by double-potting: placing pots in larger pots, urns or high-sided plant troughs and packing the space between inner and outer containers with sphagnum moss, peat moss, or vermiculite that is kept constantly moist.

For plants that require special humidity or temperature conditions, some indoor gardeners add an extra greenhouse unit, or enclose a section of their garden room by means of a glass partition and door (sold by many greenhouse manufacturers) in order to maintain different atmospheres for different groups of plants. This second, often smaller, area can serve either as a "hot house" for heat-loving tropical plants, or a "cool house" for species that prefer lower temperatures at night. It doesn't have to be kept as neat and presentable as the main garden room: it can be a functional, cluttered workplace if necessary, with regular greenhouse growing benches and a coarse gravel floor for good drainage. When in flower, prized plants can be brought into the main garden room from this separate area, or enjoyed anywhere else in the house temporarily, then returned to the con-ditions in which they grow best.

A cool or intermediate garden room is an ideal place to force normally spring-flowering bulbs into bloom during late fall and winter months, assuring a spectacular display of color year round. Most nurseries and garden mail-order catalogs offer a wide variety of tazetta narcissuses, daffodils, tulips, hyacinths, crocuses, lilies of the valley, bulbous irises, freesias, squills, and other bulbs recommended for forcing. The tall, spectacular amaryllis prefer warmer night temperatures of 60 to 65 degrees but are well worth providing for; they put on a striking display and, unlike most bulbs, can be brought into bloom year after year.

Although often overlooked, continuously flowering, easy-to-grow annuals and winter-tender perennials can be planted in a cool or intermediate garden room. Marigolds, petunias, caldendulas, salpiglosses, sweet peas, stock, and many others normally bloom outdoors in summer but can be planted indoors in summer or fall to bloom during the winter months. If you like color, a few accents or banked masses of annuals can turn January into July in a garden room.

Not least of all, a garden room maintained at less than tropical conditions can be a congenial home for any number of handsome perennial shrubs, vines, and small trees prized for their foliage and/or blossoms. While space makes it impossible to mention all of them, some of the best, and most distinctive, of these ornamental plants are described below. New, improved varieties of many of these species are constantly being developed and introduced. The specialized plant societies or house-plant sources listed under "Sources of Supply" in the back of this book can supply current information about these varieties.

Tending plants in a garden room is not a complex chore; it relies on common sense as much as anything else. A good guide to houseplants or greenhouse gardening will provide details on the individual needs of various species for watering, fertilizing, soil mixtures, pruning, propagating, and repotting.

Generally speaking, plant growth slows in winter with the diminishing of natural light; in midwinter most plants need a period of rest, and many flowering species also require cool conditions in order to set flower buds. During this period plants should be watered and fertilized more sparingly than when they are in active growth. Under warm, sunny conditions, plants absorb more moisture through their roots and transpire it through their leaves, and thus need more frequent watering, but they need less water when days are cloudy or cool.

Overwatering is the greatest enemy of any plant grown indoors. While most plants can tolerate a dry spell, few can survive drowning: the excess water a plant is unable to absorb simply waterlogs the soil, cutting off vital air and rotting the roots. Make a habit of checking your plants regu-

larly, at least once every three days. Most plants should be watered only when the top of the soil is a light, sandy brown or feels dry, or when the pot seems unusually light. The oldest, and best, rule of thumb about watering is when in doubt, don't.

Plants are more tolerant of various conditions than one might imagine. Night temperatures specified in the entries below indicate a general, ideal range for different species. (If a particular figure doesn't meet with your personal experience, re-

member that there are almost as many opinions on temperatures, and other gardening matters, as there are experts—and that gardening is still less of a science than it is an art.) A plant may be able to stand a drop below the lower figure noted without any ill effects, though if repeatedly subjected to temperatures much lower than desirable it may yellow, shed its leaves or drop its flower buds. Most plants won't do well if daytime temperatures are allowed to climb beyond 80 or 85 degrees, and they

grow about 2 feet high and are usually covered with dozens of small single or double blossoms. Pericat azaleas, *R. pericat*, are similar in size but bear larger blossoms, and Rutherford azaleas, *R. rutherfordiana*, produce still more spectacular blooms up to 3 inches across. Other varieties include *R. jasminiflorum*, which has small, white, jasmine-like flowers. All like a sunny spot in winter and bright indirect light the rest of the year, a relatively high humidity of 60 percent, and cool night temperatures of 45 to 55 degrees.

BEGONIA
Begonia

Among the most popular and varied species for garden rooms, begonias range from flowering plants grown mainly for their foliage to large-flowered varieties that come in brilliant colors of almost every hue. Rex or fancy-leaved begonias (*B. rex*), when massed in groups, make a striking display with their tapestry-patterned, 8- to 12-inch leaves, in mixed shades of green, red, pink, silver, and bronze. Rieger begonias (*B. elatior*) are smaller plants that bear a profusion of pink, red, white, yellow, or orange blossoms; a fine trailing type with large double flowers is 'Aphrodite Pink'. Wax begonias (*B. semperflorens*) have smaller but abundant red, pink, or white flowers throughout the year. Showiest of all are tuberous begonias (*B. tuberhybrida*), which boast blossoms 8 inches across, some resembling large roses

Loose clusters of distinctive blossoms resembling tiny trumpets adorn *Rhododendron jasminiflorum*, an unusual species originally imported from Malaya, where it often grows on trees as an epiphyte or "air plant". The flowers have a sweet fragrance, like that of narcissus.

Tuberous begonias, with their generous blossoms, lend bold splashes of color to almost any interior scheme. Largely native to Central and South America, begonias come in an extravagant range of types and colors, comprising one of the largest family of flowering plants that can be grown in a garden room.

or camellias in dazzling colors that make dramatic accents. Upright types grow 1½ to 2 feet tall, while trailing varieties with stems 4 to 5 feet long make fine hanging plants.

Wax, Rieger, and tuberous begonias prefer direct sunlight in winter but filtered sun the rest of the year; rex begonias need partial shade year round. All like intermediate to warm night temperatures of 55 to 65 degrees. Begonias prefer a relatively high humidity of 60 percent or more but need good air circulation to avoid mildew.

BIRD-OF-PARADISE FLOWER
Strelitzia

Few indoor plants are as striking in bloom as *S. reginae*, which when mature has broad, spear-shaped leaves several feet high and bears tall-stalked, orange-and-blue flowers. A dwarf variety, *humilis*, grows only about 1½ feet high and is suited to limited spaces. For good blooming, strelitzias need direct sun (except during hot midsummer days) and intermediate night temperatures of 50 to 55 degrees.

BLACK-EYED-SUSAN VINE, CLOCK VINE
Thunbergia

A colorful vine for a hanging basket or trellis, *T. alata* produces wiry stems up to 4 feet long bearing small, heart-shaped leaves and dozens of orange-, yellow-, buff-, or white-petalled flowers that open to the sun to reveal black or purple "eyes." Thunbergias like direct sun and intermediate night temperatures of 50 to 60 degrees.

BOUGAINVILLEA
Bougainvillea

Gently evocative of the Old South, these lush, fast-growing tropical vines can climb 6 feet or more. Their brilliant clusters of flowery bracts in shades of bright purple, red, pink, magenta, orange, yellow, and white provide almost continuous color for a garden room corner and are often most dramatic when kept pruned. Recent hybrids bred for more compact growth include 'Texas Dawn' (pink) and 'Spectabilis' (purple), both about 2 feet tall. Give bougainvilleas direct sun and intermediate to warm night temperatures of 55 to 65 degrees.

BROWALLIA
Browallia

Almost constantly in bloom, browallias make attractive hanging basket plants, their delicate five-petalled flowers up to 2 inches across blooming on spreading, trailing stems up to 3 feet in length. Most hybrids have blue flowers, except for a favorite variety, *B. speciosa major*, which has either blue or white flowers, and the white-blossomed 'Silver Bells'. Plants grow best in direct sun in winter, indirect light the rest of the year. Night temperatures should be an intermediate 55 to 60 degrees.

CAMELLIA
Camellia

For some the most romantic of flowers, camellias bloom in midwinter and are available in many splendid varieties lending vivid pink, red, or white accents to any grouping of plants. Shrubs with dark evergreen leaves, they are usually pruned to a height of 2 or 3 feet. *C. japonica*, the common camellia, has blossoms up to 5 inches across that resemble peonies, those of the netvein camellia, *C. retitulata*, are even larger, up to 7 inches across. The sasanqua camellia, *C. sasanqua*, is a daintier species with 2-inch flowers that look like wild roses. Camellias thrive in filtered sunlight (some direct sun in winter), high humidity of 60 percent or more, and good air movement. They like cool night temperatures, which can fall as low as 40 degrees, and day temperatures below 70.

The vivid, pinkish red blossom of a *Camellia japonica* variety named 'Adolphe Audusson' resembles a large peony. The species, native to Japan and China, has been extensively hybridized, and many other varieties are available. Camellias make handsome accent shrubs, flowering for four to six weeks in winter in a cool garden room.

'Joanmarie Shelton' is one of a long roster of gorgeous cattleya orchids favored by indoor gardening amateurs. Typical of cattleyas is the large, ruffled lip, or lower petal. Varieties include not only white but a rainbow of other hues and color combinations, ranging from yellows and oranges to greens and blues.

CAPE COWSLIP
Lachenalia

One of the more unusual bulbs for forcing, Cape cowslips not only have vivid flowers that last up to two months, they are also easy to grow and, unlike most other bulbs, can be brought to bloom again in following years. Each bulb sends up one or two spikes less than a foot high, bearing flaming clusters of tubular flowers in shades of yellow, orange, or red, depending on the variety. Cape cowslips need full sun and prefer cool night temperatures of 40 to 50 degrees and day temperatures of 60 degrees or less.

CATTLEYA ORCHID
Cattleya

These classic corsage orchids come in literally thousands of hybrids and every color of the rainbow. Easy orchids for beginners to grow in a garden room, they yield showy flowers up to 7 inches across on 1- to 1½-foot stems, some as often as three times a year. Good choices for limited spaces are the newer, more compact "mini-catts". Cattleyas like intermediate to warm night temperatures of 55 to 65 degrees, bright indirect sunlight, and a humidity of 50 to 60 percent.

CLIVIA, KAFIR LILY
Clivia

Eye-catching accents in a garden room, clivias or Kafir lilies send up brilliantly colored clusters of 10 to 20 trumpet-shaped flowers atop foot-high stalks, which emerge from the arching, strap-shaped leaves. *C. miniata* has yellow-throated orange to red blossoms, followed by decorative red berries; those of *C. cyrtanthiflora* are salmon pink. Clivias flourish in bright indirect light and intermediate night temperatures of 50 to 60 degrees.

COLEUS
Coleus

Planted in low masses, the deep maroon, green, yellow, and pink leaves of coleus provide an enhancing background for taller plants. Common coleus, *C. blumei*, forms a bush up to 2 or 3 feet high. Rehnelt coleus, *C. rehneltianus*, is a trailing plant available in several fine varieties, including 'Trailing Queen' (red, yellow, and purple) and 'Lord Falmouth' (pink and red). Coleuses prefer sun and warm night temperatures of 65 to 70 degrees.

CYCLAMEN
Cyclamen

C. persicum, the familiar florists' cyclamen, is generally bought when it starts to bloom in early fall. It will grow about a foot high and bear dozens of 2- to 3-inch crimson, magenta, pink, or white flowers that seem to hover like butterflies above decorative heart-shaped foliage; some varieties have bicolored blooms or silver-marked leaves. The tall-stalked blossoms, fragrant in certain varie-

The clivia, or Kafir lily, native to South Africa, puts on a splendid show of lily-like blossoms above sword-shaped, waxy leaves. The colors of different species and varieties include orange-red, yellow, pink, and white. All make fine cut flowers or potted plants for display.

Highly decorative foliage plants, including coleuses and caladiums demonstrate that a garden room need not rely entirely on flowers for colorful effects. Here they are combined with the pink blossoms of wax begonias and the paler pink blooms of annual impatiens.

ties, also make handsome and long-lasting cut flowers. For continuous winter blossoming, cyclamens need full sun or bright indirect light, ample humidity and ventilation, and cool night temperatures of 40 to 55 degrees at night and 50 to 60 degrees during the day.

CYMBIDIUM ORCHID
Cymbidium

Among the most popular orchids, cymbidiums bear arching sprays of waxy, long-lasting flowers, which range in color from pale ivory to deep yellow, chartreuse, and mahogany. Standard hybrids have stems up to 3 feet long and do best in cool night temperatures of 45 to 50 degrees (60 degrees in summer); miniatures grow about a foot high and can tolerate the same temperatures but prefer an intermediate 50 to 60 degrees.

DENDROBIUM ORCHID
Dendrobium

Bearing large, graceful blooms, dendrobiums come in many spectacular species and varieties, in all sizes and colors. Evergreen types like night temperatures of 60 degrees; deciduous ones prefer a cool 50 degrees during their winter dormancy and an intermediate 55 to 60 when growing and flowering. Both grow best in direct sun or bright indirect light.

EPIDENDRUM ORCHID
Epidendrum

These orchids come in hundreds of varieties that make lovely pot or hanging basket plants. The many hybrids of *E. ibaguense* bear clusters of tiny 1- to 3-inch flowers on 2- to 4-foot stems; the clamshell orchid, *E. cochleatum*, has delicately scented blooms which hang upside down on short stems; the diminutive *E. mariae* grows only 6 to 8 inches high. Most epidendrums like bright indirect light and intermediate night temperatures of 50 to 60 degrees.

EUROPEAN FAN PALM
Chamaerops

Distinctive among palms for its stiff, fan-shaped fronds, which can reach 6 feet in height, *C. humilis* acts as a strong focal point in a garden room. It thrives in intermediate night temperatures of 50 to 55 degrees and bright indirect light, but can take full sun in winter.

FLAMING SWORD, PAINTED FEATHER
Vriesia

Among the many tropical bromeliads, the arching foliage and showy blossoms of vriesias lend special color to a garden room. *V. splendens* is notable for its blue-green leaves striped with purple, and its fiery red-and-yellow flower spikes which bloom in spring and summer, prompting its common name, flaming sword. *V. guttata*, known as painted feather, produces clusters of pale yellow blooms from late winter to early summer. Both grow to about a foot tall. They do best in bright indirect sun and warm night temperatures of 60 to 70 degrees.

FLOWERING MAPLE
Abutilon

Prized for their constant displays of bell-shaped flowers, abutilons are not true maples, but tropical plants with maple-like leaves. Bushy varieties, which can grow 5 or 6 feet tall unless pruned, include *A. striatum thompsonii*, with orange-pink blossoms, *A. hybridum* 'Golden Fleece', with yellow flowers, and other hybrids with white, pink, or purple blooms. *A. megapotamicum variegatum*, with red-and-yellow flowers on long, trailing stems, is ideal for hanging baskets. All like direct sun (light shade in summer) and intermediate night temperatures of 55 to 60 degrees.

FREESIA
Freesia

Classic greenhouse plants, freesias produce exquisite sprays of spicily fragrant, trumpet-shaped blossoms on 1- to 1½-foot stems through winter and early spring. The original wild

A fuchsia hybrid displays the species' characteristically graceful "hoop-skirt" blooms. The sepals flare upward to reveal hanging, bell-like flowers with long anthers that suggest a dancer's legs.

species, native to South Africa, have yellow and red blossoms, and are available in many hybrids with colors ranging from white to pink, red, lilac, and blue (although some of the larger-flowered hybrids have less scent). Freesias like plenty of sun and cool to intermediate temperatures, 45 to 55 degrees at night.

FUCHSIA
Fuchsia

Among the loveliest of flowering plants, fuchsias come in several thousand varieties, from upright shrubs and standards to trailing basket plants, with flowers in various combinations of pink, red, orange, purple, and white. Without added artificial light most bloom only during the long daylight of spring and summer, but some "everbloomers" will flower in normal winter day lengths under optimum growing conditions. These include trailing varieties like 'Mrs. Victor Reiter', which has single red-and-white flowers; 'Cascade', dark pink; and 'Abundance', with double pink blooms. A bush type that blooms year round is *F. triphylla*, the honey-suckle fuchsia. Fuchsias like full sun in winter and intermediate night temperatures of 50 to 55 degrees. In summer, keep plants cool and moist in a shady outdoor spot.

GARDENIA, CAPE JASMINE
Gardenia

Gardenias aren't the easiest plants to bring to flower indoors—many houses

are just too warm and dry for their tastes—but the reward repays the effort: smooth, creamy white blooms with a heady scent. *G. jasminoides vetchii*, named for its jasmine-like aroma, is a handsome plant with dark evergreen leaves and grows up to 3 feet tall to produce stunning 3-inch flowers; blooms of cultivars like 'Belmont', 'Hadley', 'Mystery' and 'McLellan 23' can reach 5 inches in diameter. A new cultivar named 'Golden Magic' has yellow flowers—for gardenias, a real conversation piece. Gardenias must have plenty of sun and moisture to blossom; give them a room humidifier or a pebble tray with water and keep night temperatures at an intermediate 50 to 55 degrees. They won't set new flower buds if night temperatures go much over 60 degrees.

GERANIUM
Pelargonium

Geraniums add a dash of color to garden rooms, and the more sun they get the more they will provide their cheerful hues month after month. The most familiar are the widely available hybrids of *P. hortorum*, sometimes called the common, house or zonal geranium, which blooms indoors from late winter to fall in white, pink, red, or lavender; the leaves of different varieties are marked with concentric bands of white, yellow, brown, or red. Also popular are the large-flowered Lady Washington or regal geraniums (*P. domesticum*) and the

scented geraniums (many species and varieties), which bloom in spring and have lemon-, pine-, apple-, rose-, or peppermint-scented leaves which can be used to flavor beverages and foods. Good choices for hanging baskets are varieties of the ivy geranium, *P. peltatum*, which bear smaller clusters of blossoms on trailing stems from late spring to fall. Geraniums prefer intermediate night temperatures of 50 to 55 degrees but tolerate up to 65 degrees.

GLORY BOWER
Clerodendrum

These vigorous tropical species, which flower abundantly, can be pruned to bushy plants for pots or left to grow freely in hanging baskets or on trellises. *C. thomsoniae*, a twining vine, is also called bleeding heart for its blood-red flowers which grow out of white calyxes. *C. fragrans pleniflorum*, a 3- to 5-foot shrub, bears clusters of pink and white, hyacinth-scented blossoms, and the smaller *C. fallax* has brilliant red blooms. Clerodendrums do best in full sun (light shade in summer) and intermediate to warm night temperatures of 60 to 65 degrees; under these conditions they can bloom year-round.

Geraniums, among the easiest-to-grow and most popular of houseplants, belong to a large family of species that originated in South Africa. They come in myriad forms beside the standard windowbox variety. Here, 'Ballerina', a pale pink cultivar, is grown as an upright standard on a single stalk.

GLOXINIA
Sinningia

Hybrids of *S. speciosa* resemble African violets but bear larger, ruffled flowers 3 to 6 inches across more suitable for groupings with larger plants and shrubs. Gloxinias bloom at various times, in shades of white, pink, lavender, red, and purple sometimes marked with contrasting hues. Miniatures like *S. pusilla* grow only a couple of inches high but will produce flowers an inch or less across throughout the year. Gloxinias like bright indirect light and miniatures in particular appreciate high humidity. Night temperatures are ideal at a warm 65 to 70 degrees, but can go as low as 55.

HOYA, WAX PLANT
Hoya

These twining vines, which have glossy, oval leaves 2 to 4 inches long, produce tiny clusters of fragrant, long-lasting flowers with a waxy texture. Most common is *H. carnosa*, bearing pale pink, red-centered blossoms through summer and fall; among others, a dwarf species, *H. bella*, has red-centered white flowers. Plants flourish in diffused light and will tolerate direct sun. Optimum night temperatures are an intermediate 50 to 55 degrees.

One of the most beautiful members of the jasmine family is the primrose jasmine, *Jasminum mesnyi*. This plant, grown as a small tree in an ornamental urn, forms a fountain-like spray of yellow flowers on long, trailing stems.

JASMINE
Jasminum

The heady fragrance of even a small jasmine plant in bloom is enough to perfume an entire room. Royal jasmine, *J. gracile magnificum*, bears 1-inch white blossoms in winter; *J. polyanthum* has small white and pink flowers from late winter to late spring; *J. mesnyi*, primrose jasmine, produces larger yellow blossoms in spring. Jasmines can be pruned to remain pot plants but their inclination is to spread and they can be used in hanging baskets or trained on trellises. They need full sun and intermediate night temperatures of 50 to 55 degrees.

CAROLINA JASMINE
Gelsemium

A vine for winter and early spring color, *G. sempervirens* bears clusters of fragrant, small yellow flowers among its shiny, willow-like leaves. Plants do best in full sun and intermediate night temperatures of 50 to 55 degrees.

LIPSTICK PLANT, BASKETVINE
Aeschyanthus

Good hanging species for a warm, moist garden room, lipstick plants are named for their vivid orange-red or yellow tubular flowers, 2 to 4 inches long, which bloom on trailing stems with dark, waxy leaves. A fine hybrid is 'Black Pagoda', which produces brown-speckled, yellow-and-green flowers throughout the year.

Provide warm night temperatures of 65 to 70 degrees, a relatively high humidity of 50 to 60 percent and bright sun in winter (light shade the rest of the year).

MONSTERA, SWISS CHEESE PLANT
Monstera

If you want a bold "jungle" look, *M. deliciosa* is ready to deliver: often misleadingly sold as "split-leaf philodendrons" when young, at maturity the plants sport broad, glossy green leaves up to a foot long that are deeply notched and perforated, giving rise to the name "Swiss cheese plant." A naturally vining species, it is usually grown in a tub and given a slab of wood on which to climb, it sometimes reaches a height of 6 feet or more. Monsteras like bright indirect sunlight and warm night temperatures of 60 to 70 degrees; they will tolerate 60 or less but at the expense of new growth (which is one way of keeping them within bounds).

NORFOLK ISLAND PINE
Araucaria

A. heterophylla is a distinctively handsome, upright evergreen, with whorls of drooping, needled branches; it is sometimes sold as an exotic Christmas tree, but it makes a good background plant in almost any garden room. Though it grows to 200 feet on its native South Pacific island, it seldom reaches more than 6 or 8 feet indoors; a compact form named 'Grac-

ilis' is even smaller. Norfolk Island pine does well in bright indirect light, but will tolerate dim light and can take full sun in winter; it does best in intermediate night temperatures of 50 to 55 degrees but can stand 45 degrees.

OLEANDER, ROSEBAY
Nerium

The lovely, delicately scented, white, yellow, pink, or red blossoms of oleander adds old-fashioned romance to any garden room. Available in both single-and double-flowered varieties, these long-leaved evergreen shrubs will readily grow 2 to 5 feet high indoors. They normally bloom from early summer to fall and rest in winter with cool night temperatures of 45 to 50 degrees. But if night temperatures are maintained at 60 degrees or higher, they may bloom intermittently, or even continuously, through the winter months. For good flowering, give them plenty of sun. Oleanders should be avoided in households where small children like to experiment by eating things: their leaves, buds, and flowers are extremely poisonous.

PARADISE PALM, SENTRY PALM
Howeia (or Kentia)

Handsome upright palms, howeias are slow growers but live for many years. The paradise palm, *H. fosteriana*, forms an open, vase-shaped crown

up to 10 feet tall; the sentry palm, *H. belmoreana*, is somewhat more compact. They do best in partial shade and warm night temperatures of 60 to 65 degrees.

PARLOR PALM BAMBOO PALM
Chamaedorea

In the limited space of most garden rooms, palms are best used as background plantings, and these varieties are well-suited for a shady back wall or corner. The parlor palm, *C. elegans*, has arching, feathery fronds and grows 1 to 3 feet tall; the bamboo palm, *C. erumpens*, has upright bamboo-like stems that can rise to 8 feet. Both like warm night temperatures of 60 to 70 degrees but will tolerate 50 to 60 degrees.

JAPANESE PITTOSPORUM
Pittosporum

P. tobira, with its handsome, dark green, rhododendron-like leaves, is the kind of worthy but unsung background plant that will live for years under almost any conditions indoors. Mature plants, which grow more than 3 feet tall unless pruned, bear fragrant clusters of tiny, white, or yellow flowers in spring. Pittosporums prefer full sun but will grow in bright indirect light. Ideal night temperatures in winter are a cool 40 to 55 degrees but plants will stand warmer temperatures.

PLUMBAGO, LEADWORT
Plumbago

These attractive flowering shrubs are at their best when their long branches, which can reach several feet in length, are trained to trellises or wires inside a garden room. From spring through fall, *P. capensis* (also called *P. auriculata*) bears loose clusters of small, phlox-like blossoms that are a pale, heavenly blue; the blooms of *P. capensis alba* are white. Both like full sun and will grow in intermediate night temperatures of 50 to 60 degrees, but will flower earlier and longer if temperatures are kept above 60 or 65 degrees.

PODOCARPUS,
JAPANESE YEW
Podocarpus

The Chinese or shrubby podocarpus, *P. macrophyllus maki*, is a graceful, durable evergreen tree whose flat, needle-like leaves are bright green when young, dark green as they mature, making a striking color combination on the same plant. It may grow 6 feet high or more indoors but can be pinched back to form a smaller, bushier specimen of almost any size. Another fine choice is the fern pine, *P. gracilior*. Plants prefer bright indirect light but will grow in full sun or deep shade. Night temperatures should be on the cool side: 45 to 55 degrees.

Climbing vines adorn the interior of a garden room and filter hot summer sun. This plumbago, trained to an archway, displays clusters of small, sky-blue blossoms overhead.

An obconica primrose is one of a number of varieties whose flowers range from white to pink, lavender, and red. Descendants of a Chinese species, they bloom in winter and thus are good choices among primroses for a garden room. Plants can be used singly, but are most effective in an interior planting scheme when half a dozen or more are massed.

PRIMROSE
Primula

The large family of primroses includes many small plants with beautifully colored flowers that come into their own when seen in the close quarters of a conservatory. Fairy primroses, *P. malacoides*, bear clusters of small white, pink, or red flowers on stems less than a foot tall and may stay in bloom for three or four months. The obconica primrose, *P. obconica*, has larger flowers that also come in lavender; the polyanthus primrose, *P. polyanthus*, is a smaller plant that adds yellow and purple to the spectrum. All primroses like bright indirect sun and cool temperatures of 40 to 50 degrees at night and 50 to 60 degrees during the day.

ROSE
Rosa

Not everyone realizes that roses can be grown indoors, but under the right conditions they will blossom virtually year round and tend to be less troubled by pests than outdoors. Good choices, especially if space is limited, are the many varieties of miniature roses. Most grow about a foot high and bear flowers the size of a quarter or less, in the same rainbow palette of larger roses: white, pink, yellow, orange, red, and exquisite combinations of these colors. For maximum flower production, give roses as much sun as possible but not a great deal of heat, and intermediate night temperatures of 50 to 60 degrees.

SILK OAK
Grevillea

Looking more like a fern than an oak, this small tree will provide a lacy accent in a sunny spot where shade-loving ferns won't do well. *G. robusta*, as its name implies, is a robust plant that may grow a foot or more a year but can be pruned to remain at an appropriate height indoors. Keep night temperatures at an intermediate 50 to 55 degrees.

YESTERDAY, TODAY AND TOMORROW, CHAMELEON PLANT
Brunfelsia

B. calycina is nicknamed for its fragrant 1- to 2-inch flowers, which turn from dark purple to lavender to white on successive days. It prefers direct sun in winter, light shade in summer, and intermediate night temperatures of 50 to 55 degrees.

Fern Gardens

Ever since Victorian times, when no parlor was considered complete without one, ferns have been universal indoor favorites. And while varieties of the famous Boston fern continue to dominate the best-seller list, there are many others of different sizes, shapes, and leaf patterns to choose from.

Ferns are generally undemanding plants, preferring dappled sun or light shade and moist, cool air similar to conditions in their natural forest habitats. They do best toward the rear of a garden room where direct sun penetrates only a few hours a day, if at all, and where they will be out of drafts.

To give ferns the high humidity they prefer, set them on or above shallow trays filled with gravel and enough water to keep the gravel constantly moist. Ferns also take to bathrooms and kitchens where humidity is generally higher than the rest of the house, and to a garden room that has a fountain or pool. Good companion plants for the tropical ferns, because they thrive in the same conditions of indirect light and high humidity, are many kinds of orchids and bromeliads, which will provide colorful flowers against the lacy foliage. If maintaining high humidity is a problem, ferns that tolerate drier air include the mother fern (*Asplenium bulbiferum*), the holly fern (*Cyrtomium falcatum*), and the polypodiums.

ASPARAGUS FERN
Asparagus

Relatives of the garden vegetable, asparagus ferns are technically not ferns at all but are nevertheless old favorites as houseplants. Best known is the Sprenger asparagus fern, *A. sprengeri*, a fine hanging plant that forms billows of flat, bright green needles on arching stems generally 1½ to 2 feet long. The many-branched asparagus fern, *A. myriocladus*, has dark green needles on zig-zagging branchlets and stems that may grow 4 to 6 feet long; the twisted asparagus fern, *A. retrofractus*, is similar with bright green needles. The foxtail asparagus fern, *A. meyerii*, gets its name from upright, furry plumes 1 to 2 feet long. All grow well in partial shade and intermediate night temperatures of 50 to 55 degrees.

BOSTON FERN, SWORD FERN
Nephrolepis

The familiar Boston fern, *N. exaltata bostoniensis*, is a mutation of the sword fern and in turn has sired numerous mutations of its own. Commonly grown is the dwarf Boston fern (*compacta*), whose 1½-foot fronds are about half as long as the standard Boston. Varieties with curling or lacy foliage include 'Fluffy Ruffles', 'Mini-Ruffle', 'Verona', *Childsii*, and *Whitmanii*. All grow well in low to bright indirect light and intermediate to warm night temperatures of 50 to 70 degrees.

BRAKE FERN, TABLE FERN
Pteris

Brake ferns are popular as small house or "table" plants for their varied fronds, which seldom grow more than 1 foot long. The Cretan brake fern or ribbon fern, *P. cretica*, comes in several varieties: dark green leaflets striped cream-white, light green leaflets frilled on the edges, light green leaflets divided into fan-shaped tips. The sword brake fern, *P. ensiformis*, is prized for its variety *victoriae*, which has distinctive silvery fronds edged in dark green. The crested spider brake fern, *P. multifida cristata*, has frilly clusters at the ends of its fronds. The trembling brake fern, *P. tremula*, has feathery light green fronds that can grow up to 3 feet long. All thrive in low light and intermediate night temperatures of 50 to 55 degrees.

CHRISTMAS FERN, POLYSTICHUM FERN
Polystichum

The Christmas fern, *P. acrostichoides*, is a common evergreen fern native to eastern North American woodlands; it also makes a handsome houseplant, with its upright 1- to 3-foot fronds bearing dark green 3-inch leaflets sometimes likened to angels' wings. Among other species, the western sword fern, *P. munitum*, has longer, daggerlike leaflets with spiny edges. Smaller types include the English hedge fern, *P. setiferum*, which grows up to 1½ feet tall, and the Tsussima holly fern, *P. tsus-simense*, 1 foot high or less. All do well in low to bright indirect light and intermediate night temperatures of 50 to 55 degrees.

DAVALLIA
Davallia

Davallias, which come in various species, are small epiphytes or air plants that grow 1 to 1½ feet tall from furry

Boston ferns, classic conservatory plants since Victorian days, are often suspended in hanging containers, but this one is given special prominence on a pedestal of its own. Prone to chance mutations of frilled or twisted fronds, by the early 1900s Boston ferns had become available in some 75 varieties, though only about 20 or so of the most popular ones are still cultivated today.

rhizomes resembling animal paws; they are particularly attractive placed on slabs of bark or in hanging baskets. Davallias tolerate varying degrees of shade and like intermediate to warm night temperatures of 50 to 70 degrees.

HOLLY FERN
Cyrtomium

The holly fern, *C. falcatum*, has dark, lustrous, arching fronds 1 to 2 feet long composed of pointed 3- to 5-inch leaflets resembling holly leaves. The variety called *caryotideum* has drooping leaflets with saw-toothed edges, and *rochefordianum* has wider leaflets with wavy, toothed edges. These plants prefer shade and intermediate night temperatures of 50 to 60 degrees but will stand temperatures as low as 35.

MAIDENHAIR FERN
Adiantum

Maidenhairs are widely popular for their clouds of dainty leaflets held on black, wiry stems. *A. capillus-veneris*, the southern maidenhair fern, has fronds 6 to 20 inches long with almost translucent evergreen leaves. The delta maidenhair, *A. raddianum*, also called *A. cuneatum*, has erect fronds 9 to 18 inches tall often used by florists for cut greens (among many varieties, a favorite is the feathery 'Goldelse'). *A. tenerum*, the delicate maidenhair fern, has two commonly grown varieties: 'Farleyense', with arching, plumelike fronds up to 2 feet long, and *Wrightii*, of similar size with fan-shaped leaflets. Maidenhairs do best in partial shade and intermediate night temperatures of 50 to 60 degrees.

POLYPODY FERN
Polypodium

This large family includes plants of widely varying appearance. One of the most appealing, and easiest to grow indoors, is the golden polypody or rabbit's-foot fern, *P. aureum*, which has bold, leathery fronds 2 feet or more long that bear golden spores; a variety, *mandaianum*, is bluish green with twisted, toothed edges. Polypodys prefer bright indirect light and intermediate night temperatures of 50 to 60 degrees.

SPLEENWORT
Asplenium

The mother fern, *A. bulbiferum*, has feathery fronds 1 to 2 feet long; bulbs sprout on the leaves and develop into plantlets that can be potted. The Mauritius mother fern, *A. viviparum*, produces its plantlets on narrow-leaved, 1-foot fronds that trail gracefully from hanging baskets. Smaller species native to cooler North American climates are the ebony spleenwort, *A. platyneuron*, with fronds 8 inches to a foot or so long, and the maidenhair spleenwort, *A. trichomanes*, whose slender, 6-inch fronds have tiny, rounded leaflets. Unlike most ferns, the fronds of *A. nidus*, the birds-nest fern, are not divided into leaflets but are single, tongue-like leaves about a foot long that rise from a dark center resembling a bird's nest. Spleenworts like low light levels and intermediate night temperatures of 50 to 60 degrees (a cooler 45 to 55 for the ebony and maidenhair spleenworts).

The aptly named staghorn fern is a slow-growing epiphyte, or air plant, flourishing here on an upright log, as it does on trees in the tropics. Common staghorns have antler- or finger-like divisions at the end of their fronds, but one species from Angola bears huge, wedge-shaped leaves that look like elephant ears.

STAGHORN FERN
Platycerium

Unique among ferns, the epiphytic staghorns have broad, forking fronds that look very much like antlers. The most popular species is the common staghorn fern, *P. bifurcatum* (or *P. alcicorne*), whose fronds may reach 3 feet in length; it is best grown in a hanging basket or wall container, or on a slab of bark. Staghorns like bright indirect light, high humidity, and intermediate night temperatures of 50 to 55 degrees.

TREE FERN
Cibotium

Tree ferns, which can be grown in pots when young but eventually spread up to 6 feet across, are exotic choices if you have the space for them. Hawaiian tree ferns, *C. glaucum* and *C. menziesii*, are often sold as leafless, rootless trunks and sprout fronds that attain lengths of 4 to 6 feet. The Mexican tree fern, *C. schiedei*, forms a fountain of fronds 3 or 4 feet high and 6 feet in diameter. *C. barometz*, Scythian lamb, has 4- to 5-foot fronds that are fragrant and hairy. Tree ferns like bright indirect sun and intermediate night temperatures of 50 to 60 degrees.

A Cactus and Succulent Garden

Cacti and succulents are favored choices for those with a brown thumb or a peripatetic lifestyle. They require little care, can be extremely long-lived, are easy for beginners to grow, even on an ordinary windowsill, and being slow growers are not likely to exceed their allotted bounds. But they will positively thrive—and many of them will bloom spectacularly—in a garden room offering optimum conditions of temperature, ventilation, and light. Cacti and succulents range in size from 1 to 2 inches to several feet high. Larger plants make striking individual accents; smaller ones often look best grouped in a shallow container or dish garden.

Most species like full sun but some sensitive ones should be shaded, especially in summer, to prevent scorching. Good air movement is essential, particularly during hot weather, as even desert plants can stifle in oppressive heat. Cacti generally need to dry out thoroughly between waterings, a condition easier to maintain and judge if they are in ordinary, porous clay pots rather than plastic or glazed ceramic containers. From November through February, those species that go into semidormancy should be watered even less, only once every few weeks, just enough to keep them from shriveling. Succulents not native to desert climates, such as the Christmas cactus (*Schlumbergera bridgesii*), need more regular watering, so that the soil around them becomes only moderately dry.

The following are a few of the more popular cacti and succulents for indoor growing.

ALOE
Aloe

Aloes form fleshy, pointed spears, sometimes marked with contrasting colors. The true aloe, *A. vera*, is sometimes grown on kitchen windowsills because its leaves when cut exude a fluid that soothes scrapes and burns; these pale green leaves may eventually reach a length of 1½ to 2 feet. The most attention-getting species is the tiger aloe, *A. variegata*, whose leaves have white-spotted bands and form a mound that may grow 1 foot tall and 6 inches across. Aloes like sun and intermediate night temperatures of 50 to 55 degrees.

CHRISTMAS CACTUS, EASTER CACTUS, THANKSGIVING CACTUS
Schlumbergera

These cacti, named for their approximate blooming seasons, bear blossoms at the tips of arching, crablike branches up to 1½ feet long that make them particularly effective in hanging baskets. The Christmas cactus, *S. bridgesii*, usually has red flowers but hybrids are multicolored or white. Blossoms are scarlet in the case of the Easter cactus, *S. gaertneri*, (also called *Rhipsalidopsis gaertneri*), and rose pink in the Thanksgiving cactus, *S. truncata* (also called *Zygocactus truncatus*). Before blooming, night temperatures should be an intermediate 50 to 60 degrees. When the buds set, keep night temperatures at a warmer 60 to 70 degrees.

EASTER LILY CACTUS
Echinopsis

Small, round, vertically ribbed cacti that flower when only about 3 inches in diameter, echinopsis bear pink, orange, and yellow blossoms that open at night and are often as large as the plants themselves. The Easter lily cactus, *E. multiplex*, also called *Cereus multiplex*, has fragrant, pink, lilylike blooms up to 6 inches across. All like sun or bright indirect light and cool night temperatures of 40 to 45 degrees in winter.

ECHEVERIA
Echeveria

Most echeverias are favored for indoor dish gardens because they form low rosettes of succulent leaves a few inches across, sometimes sending up slender stems topped by clusters of tiny pink, red, or yellow flowers. Painted lady (*E. derenbergii*) has pale green leaves edged in red; the peacock echeveria (*E. peacockii*) has matte silver-blue leaves with red edges and tips; the plush plant (*E. pulvinata*) is densely covered with small white hairs. Echeverias like sun (except the plush plant, which prefers bright indirect light or partial shade) and intermediate night temperatures of 50 to 55 degrees.

A jade plant, the undersides of whose leaves are a lovely green, has the naturally picturesque look of a Japanese bonsai, and thus makes a fine miniature tree indoors. Older specimens like this one are sometimes covered with white or pink blooms.

Euphorbia milii splendens, a succulent more commonly known as crown of thorns, is named for its sharp, inch-long spines and small red, pink, or yellow flowers, which bloom virtually throughout the year.

EPIPHYLLUM, ORCHID CACTUS
Epiphyllum

The many hybrids of epiphyllums—which are tree-dwelling epiphytes—produce spectacular flowers on flattened, scalloped stems off and on all year round, making fine displays for hanging baskets. *E. ackermanii*, the red orchid cactus, blooms by day, bearing 4- to 6-inch scarlet blossoms on curving stems up to 3 feet long. Varieties of *E. oxypetalum*, sometimes called queen of the night, bloom either day or night in various colors and are sweetly fragrant. They thrive in intermediate night temperatures of 50 to 55 degrees but will tolerate a wider temperature range. Unlike most cacti, epiphyllums are native to tropical rain forests and like high humidity (60 percent or more) and bright indirect or filtered sun.

EUPHORBIA
Euphorbia

This vast and varied family includes many fine plants for the garden room (including that old favorite, the Christmas poinsettia). Among the most popular of the succulent types is the crown of thorns, *E. milii splendens*, a branching, fiercely spiny shrub up to 2 or 3 feet high whose bright green leaves almost constantly bear tiny red flowers. The milk-striped euphorbia (*E. lactea*), also called dragon bones, looks like a spiky green candelabra 3 or more feet tall. The corncob euphorbia (*E. mammillaris*) is a more cactus-like plant that grows only about 8 inches high and has spiny stems that resemble green corncobs. Also aptly named is the basketball euphorbia (*E. obesa*), a pudgy 8-inch globe. Euphorbias like sun or bright indirect light, and intermediate to warm night temperatures of 55 to 65 degrees.

HAWORTHIA
Haworthia

The distinctive zebra haworthia (*H. fasciata*) is a succulent that forms a rosette of pointed 2-inch green leaves striped with lighter-colored growths called tubercles; the pearly haworthia (*H. margaritifera*) has leaves up to 3 inches long covered with a pattern of dots. Haworthias thrive in bright indirect sun and intermediate night temperatures of 50 to 55 degrees.

JADE PLANT
Crassula

Jade plants (*C. argentea*), sometimes called Chinese rubber plants, resemble miniature trees as they grow to 2 feet tall or higher, with rounded, fleshy, succulent green leaves whose edges turn red in ample sun. On certain varieties the leaves are marked with combinations of white, yellow, orange, pink, red, and purple. A cousin, the silver dollar plant (*C. arborescens*), bears gray-green leaves that have red borders and are covered with tiny red dots. All like full sun but will grow in bright indirect light or partial shade; they prefer in-

termediate night temperatures of 50 to 55 degrees but will tolerate 40 degrees.

KALANCHOE
Kalanchoe

Kalanchoes are succulents popular for their distinctively colored foliage and/or masses of tiny flowers. *K. daigremontiana* grows a foot or so tall and has blue-green leaves blotched with purple (plantlets that form on the leaves drop off and root to form a "family" around the parent). The penwiper plant, *K. marmorata*, has dense gray-green leaves spotted brownish red. The leaves of the panda or pussy-ears plant, *K. tomentosa*, are covered with silvery hairs that become brown at the tips. Among the bloomers, *K. blossfeldiana* sends up clusters of red or yellow flowers on 8-inch to 1-foot stems; other favorites are Hummel's Hybrids, which have variously colored blossoms, and Swiss Strains, whose long stems make them useful as cut flowers. Kalanchoes do best in full sun but will grow in bright indirect light; they like night temperatures at an intermediate 50 to 60 degrees.

LOBIVIA, COB CACTUS
Lobivia

Their name an anagram for their country of origin, Bolivia, lobivias are small globular or cylindrical cacti notable for their showy pink, red, or-

ange, yellow, white, lilac, or purple flowers, up to 4 inches across. Popular species include the golden Easter lily cactus, *L. aurea*, about 4 inches high bearing bright yellow, trumpet-shaped flowers, and the orange cob cactus, *L. famatimensis* (also called *Enchinocactus famatimensis*), which has purplish green stems 6 inches tall and, depending on the variety, produces blooms ranging from yellow to dark red. Lobivias like sun but will grow in bright indirect light and prefer night temperatures at a cool 40 to 45 degrees.

OLD-MAN CACTUS
Cephalocereus

Something of a conversation piece, the fat, columnar shape of *C. senilis*, less than a foot tall, is almost completely covered by long, drooping white hairs. It prefers full sun or bright indirect light, cool night temperatures of 40 to 45 degrees in winter and a warm 65 to 70 the rest of the year.

OPUNTIA CACTUS
Opuntia

The opuntias, known as prickly pears, form conglomerations of paddle-shaped stems. Bunny ears (*O. microdasys*), produces pads 3 to 6 inches long that are dotted with prickles. The beavertail cactus (*O. basilaris*), has purplish green pads 4 to 8 inches long. Both like direct sun but will tolerate a little shade and prefer cool night temperatures of 40 to 45 degrees in winter.

Kalanchoes, long popular as houseplants, will bloom even more prolifically than usual in the controlled climate of a garden room. This red-flowered hybrid is named 'Sensation'. Another favorite is 'Jingle Bells', with hanging, bell-shaped blossoms of a coral hue.

PLAID CACTUS, CHIN CACTUS
Gymnocalycium

The plaid cactus, *G. mihanovichii*, is a globular, ribbed mound 2 to 6 inches in diameter with reddish bands and icy pink flowers that appear sporadically through the year. Mutations, grafted atop other cacti and developed as cultivars, are non-flowering, but extraordinary nonetheless for their floral effect of brightly colored balls; among them are 'Red Cap', 'Orange Cap', 'Yellow Cap', and 'Pink Cap'. All grow well in sun or bright indirect light and intermediate night temperatures of 50 to 55 degrees.

QUEEN OF THE NIGHT
Selenicereus

Selenicereus grandiflora, a vine-like cactus known as queen of the night or night-blooming cereus, when mature produces huge, white, fragrant flowers that open in the evening and close by dawn. Trained along the wall and roof supports of a greenhouse, its woody, prickly stem makes an unusual cover for the framework; it is also an extraordinary addition to a conservatory used as a dining room, as its flowers scent the air with an exotic vanilla-like odor. Plants require full bright sun and night temperatures no lower than 40 degrees.

RAT-TAIL CACTUS
Aporocactus

A novel plant for a hanging basket, *A. flagelliformis*, or rattail cactus, is well-named for its tail-like stems, which are less than an inch in diameter but may grow 3 feet long, bearing a profusion of bright pink flowers in late spring. It prefers sun but will tolerate bright indirect light; ideal night temperatures are a cool 40 to 45 degrees.

SANSEVIERIA
Sansevieria

The erect, graceful leaves of these popular houseplants will tolerate almost any conditions indoors. The most familiar is the snake plant or mother-in-law tongue, *S. trifasciata* (also called *S. zebrina*), whose deep green, sword-like leaves grow 1 to 3 feet long and are handsomely patterned in lighter green or white. A variety, *laurentii*, is edged with broad yellow stripes. Newer varieties are 'Bartel's Sensation', with cream and white stripes, and *hahnii*, with gold and silver bands. Sansevierias will grow in full sun or low light. Ideal night temperatures are a warm 65 to 70 degrees, though plants can stand wide variations from this range.

SEDUM, STONECROP, BURRO'S TAIL
Sedum

This large family of succulents includes many species that can be grown indoors. Besides the small kinds, whose fleshy leaves in distinctive colors make attractive plantings for dish gardens, a favorite for hanging baskets is *S. morganianum*, the burro's or donkey's tail. An odd but rather charming plant, it has small, fat, tear-shaped leaves, covered with a blue powdery dust called bloom, which overlap in bunches to form thick, trailing stems that can grow 2 or 3 feet long. It does best in sun but will grow in bright indirect light; preferred night temperatures are an intermediate 50 to 55 degrees.

A Kitchen Garden

Many common, as well as unusual (and otherwise expensive) fruits, herbs, and vegetables can be grown indoors. Home-grown radicchio and arugula, plum tomatoes and Italian eggplant, strawberries and figs, offer great culinary and economic advantages over their store-bought brethren. Beside these benefits, there is little to compare with the pleasure of picking your own vegetables just before you're ready to eat them, especially if a February blizzard is howling outdoors.

Many plants for a kitchen garden are both ornamental and edible and so can be incorporated into any garden room planting arrangement. Grapes and figs, for example, and almost any herbs, can be vigorous and decorative additions to a foliage or flower garden.

Growing Herbs Under Glass

Clustered pots of fragrant herbs add a country elegance to any kitchen or garden room. They are among the simplest of plants to grow and, since many dried herbs are pale reflections of fresh ones, they are among the most rewarding, as well. Fresh basil or mint in winter time will evoke memories of summer, and other herbs such as lavender can be dried for scented bouquets and wreaths.

Most culinary herbs are natives of dry Mediterranean lands, where they thrive in sunshine and light, well-drained, not always highly fertile ground—conditions that can be easily duplicated in a garden room. They like to be watered only when their soil is obviously dry or when they start to wilt, and fertilized with restraint. The least demanding types—which also happen to be among the most popular—can be grown in a sunny kitchen or bedroom window, but the range of possibilities is increased considerably in the more controlled climate of a full garden room.

Some decorative plants not normally thought of as herbs make good garnishes and flavorings. Among these are the common nasturtium, *Tropaeolum majus*, a climbing garden annual whose cheery flowers can be brought to bloom in winter on trellises or in hanging containers, if given full sun and cool night temperatures of 40 to 50 degrees. Its peppery leaves are eaten like watercress and the edible blossoms—which taste much the same as the leaves and come in intense shades of cream, yellow, orange, red, or brown—lend an invigorating dash of color to salads and soups. Watercress itself, *Nasturtium officinale*, a semi-aquatic, creeping perennial, is best grown in shallow water in a large dish or around the edge of an indoor garden pool.

The foliage of many scented geraniums can also be used to decorate and flavor drinks, desserts, and other foods, or dried in fragrant potpourris. Favorites are lemon-scented geranium, *Pelargonium crispum*; peppermint-scented geranium, *P. tomentosum*; and rose-scented geranium, *P. graveolens*.

Generally speaking, herbs can stand warm day temperatures of 70 degrees or more, but need intermediate night readings of 60 degrees or less.

BASIL OR SWEET BASIL
Ocimum basilicum

A vigorous annual that thrives the more it is pinched back, basil grows 1 to 2 feet tall, or as small as 6 inches in the case of new dwarf varieties. Some cooks feel they never have enough fresh basil. Pesto requires handfuls of its leaves, and

Chives, a decorative member of the onion family, is a long-lived herb that grows well in a sunny kitchen garden room. Its leaves add zest to cold soups like vichyssoise; its delicate lavender-blue flower clusters, which have the same mild onion flavor, can be used as a colorful garnish for either salads or soups.

their clove-like flavor is so versatile that they can be used in dozens of sauces and dishes.

CHERVIL
Anthriscus cerefolium

In appearance this annual resembles parsley, and it is an herb that almost has to be used fresh to capture its delicate parsley-and-licorice flavor. Chervil grows 1 to 2 feet tall and bears clusters of tiny white flowers. It grows well in light shade.

CHIVES
Allium schoenoprasum

This long-lived perennial of the onion family has hollow, grasslike leaves, which grow in clumps 6 to 12 inches tall and have a mild onion flavor. The starry 1-inch clusters of pinkish purple flowers are highly decorative and can also be used as an edible garnish. Chives do well in sun or partial shade.

LAVENDER
Lavandula

Lacy, delicate sprays of lavender, long used in soaps and dried sachets, will lend a delightful, old-fashioned perfume to any garden room. Familiar garden species of these bushy perennials tend to be a bit tall and floppy for indoor use, so you may want to try a dwarf or compact variety instead. *L. angustifolia*, Hidcote has silvery foliage, deep purplish-blue blossoms, and rarely grows more than 1½ feet high or wide; *L. angustifolia*, Munstead is a 1-foot plant with lavender flower spikes; and Jean Davis forms mounds of blue-green leaves about 15 inches tall and bears white flowers tinged with pink. Lavenders prefer full sun and seem to be most fragrant in dry, sandy, infertile soil.

LEMON BALM
Melissa officinalis

Lemon balm, a perennial, has rounded, mint-like leaves with a distinctive lemon scent and flavor. Used in fruit and vegetable salads or iced tea, it is a pleasant change from mint. Lemon balm generally grows 1 to 2 feet tall in slowly spreading clumps and flourishes in full sun or partial shade and rather dry, infertile soil.

SWEET MARJORAM
Origanum majorana

Sweet marjoram is a perennial usually grown as an annual and can reach 2 feet. The small, oval leaves, which have a balsam-like aroma, are chopped for use in savory dishes . It prefers full sun.

MINT
Mentha

The varied mints, all vigorous perennials, are long-time favorites for their refreshingly aromatic leaves, which are most flavorful when just picked. Mint generally grows to about 2 feet tall and once established spreads rap-

'Brown Turkey', a variety of *Ficus carica*, has ornamental, deeply lobed leaves and produces quantities of delicious figs under glass, protected from birds and insects.

idly by underground roots. Familiar varieties include spearmint (*M. spicata*), which is also the most intensely flavored, white peppermint (*M. piperata officinalis*), and black peppermint (*M. piperata vulgaris*). But don't overlook apple mint, also called round-leaved or woolly mint (*M. rotundifolia*), which has an apple-like flavor, and orange or bergamot mint (*M. citra*, also known as *M. odorata*), which tastes like a cross between citrus and mint. Mint grows well in moist soil and full sun or partial shade.

PARSLEY
Petroselinum crispum

Parsley is a biennial grown for its tender first-season leaves, when plants form mounds of foliage 6 inches to 1 foot tall. Curly leaved parsley comes in several named varieties such as 'Perfection' and 'Champion Moss Curled.' Others include flat-leaved parsley like 'Plain Italian Dark Green', which tends to be more flavorful, and Hamburg or turnip-rooted parsley, whose long white roots can also be used as a vegetable. Parsley thrives in full sun but can take light shade.

ROSEMARY
Rosmarinus officinalis

Rosemary, an ornamental, evergreen perennial, is valued for its aromatic, needle-like leaves. Varieties include low-growing and prostrate types as well as some with lighter foliage and bright small blue flowers. Rosemary

should be grown in full sun.

TARRAGON OR FRENCH TARRAGON
Artemisia dracunculus

Many a neighborhood Parisian bistro serves mushrooms sauteed with tarragon, whose narrow, grey-green leaves can lend an anise flavor to anything from vegetables to vinegars. A perennial that grows in clumps 2 to 3 feet tall, tarragon likes full sun or partial shade.

THYME
Thymus

Thymes are small, wiry shrubs that grow up to 1 foot tall and produce tiny, highly aromatic leaves. The most familiar is common or garden thyme (*T. vulgaris*). Among other species, lemon thyme (*T. citriodorus*) has brighter green, lemon-scented leaves; varieties named 'Argentus' and 'Aureus' are especially ornamental with variegated and yellow leaves.

Vegetables and Fruits

A garden room is an ideal place to raise vegetables and fruits from seeds, getting a head start while the weather is still unfavorable before moving seedlings outdoors to produce early

crops. But as more people are discovering, it can also provide conditions for growing edible plants to maturity year-round.

Not all species lend themselves to indoor growing, but a surprising number do, and the most suitable "greenhouse" varieties are often marked as such in seed catalogues. Particularly appropriate are dwarf or miniature strains as well as those labeled "early"; not only can they be grown in smaller containers, saving on limited indoor space, but they tend to ripen more quickly than their standard-sized brethren. Seed catalogues list numerous small or early types of tomatoes, cabbages, and carrots, and even of such normally larger vegetables as eggplants, cucumbers, squash, and sweet corn. Also suitable for indoor cultivation are European varieties of tomatoes, cucumbers, and some vegetables that have been developed for greenhouse growing.

With enough room, regular-sized varieties can be grown in place of, or in addition to, the smaller ones, although they will most likely need larger containers, and vines will need trellises or stakes to manage their growth.

In a cool to intermediate garden room or greenhouse, where temperatures can vary from near freezing to 60 degrees, cool-season, root and leaf vegetables such as lettuce, radishes, carrots, kale, endive, shallots, peas, spinach, and Swiss chard can be easily grown. In a warm garden room, where night temperatures range from 60 to 70 degrees or higher, warm-season fruiting vegetables like tomatoes and squash can be produced as late as December and more seedlings started in midwinter to produce early crops indoors as soon as March.

Many fruits will flourish in a garden room, if they get full sun and warmth. Few people can resist the notion of eating fresh strawberries in midwinter, and they can be grown in hanging baskets, in large pots or tubs, or in strawberry urns with planting holes in the sides. Pyramidal, wooden "towers" with shelves, which come in 2- and 4-foot heights, are available at garden centers or through mail-order catalogues and are good space-saving containers for strawberries or even lettuce, herbs, and flowers. Try the full-sized, "everbearing" garden strawberries or, for a tangy treat, the smaller Alpine varieties, which are runnerless and can be easily started from seeds. Keep night temperatures above 55 degrees.

Among other fruits that grow well indoors are sweet edible figs. *Ficus carica* "Brown Turkey" is commonly available and usually produces two crops a season under glass, in addition to being a decorative foliage plant. Citrus fruits include dwarf varieties of oranges, lemons, limes, and grapefruits that grow only a few feet tall and have glossy green leaves and fragrant flowers. The popular calomondin and Otaheite varieties bear tiny, tart, decorative oranges, but some kinds bear delicious, full-sized or even over-sized fruits. *Citrus limonia ponderosa*, for example, produces quantities of edible, mild-flavored lemons that can be up to 5 inches long and weigh 3 pounds each and are particularly good for lemon pies. *C sinensis* bears full-sized oranges that make fine eating, and varieties of *C. reticulata* yield Temple oranges, Satsuma oranges and tangerines. Citrus plants should have night temperatures of 50 to 55 degrees.

More exotic fruits include kiwi (*Actinidia chinensis*), an attractive climbing shrub whose fruits taste like a cross between strawberries and bananas; kumquat (*Fortunella* species), and loquat (*Eriobotrya japonica*), ornamental evergreens whose small orange-yellow fruits can be eaten fresh or made into preserves; and such delicacies as limequats (hybrids of limes and kumquats), tangors (crosses of oranges and tangerines), and tangelos (a marriage of the grapefruit and the mandarin orange). If the garden room is warm enough (60 to 70 degrees at night), dwarf varieties of bananas like *Musa acuminata* 'Dwarf Cavendish', which grows up to 6 feet tall and yields quantities of red flowers and yellow fruits about 5 inches long can be grown. (The more common *M. coccinea* is primarily an ornamental species with bananas only 2 inches long.) Some indoor gardeners have also had success with varieties of table grapes like Muscat or Black Hamburg, with dwarf peaches and nectarines, and with such conversation-stopping, if hard-to-find, tropical fruits as bael (*Aegle marmelos*), carambola (*Averrhoa carambola*) and mangosteen (*Garcinia mangostana*).

Miniature orange trees are not only hand-some foliage plants but bear small, intensely fragrant blossoms and colorful, tart fruit.

Adding a pool or fountain to a garden creates an entirely new dimension—a fact well known to the designers of Persian gardens and Victorian conservatories alike. There is no more soothing music than the splash of a small fountain or the trickle of a miniature waterfall, nor a more exotic environment to create within the confines of a home. On a more practical level, water also raises the moisture content of the surrounding air, creating favorable conditions

Water Gardens

for ferns, orchids, and other humidity-loving plants, as well as providing a place to grow aquatic species like waterlilies.

An indoor water garden can be as simple as a concealed length of pipe from which drops of water splash slowly into a decorative basin surrounded by potted plants. With an inexpensive electric submersible pump, which recirculates water continuously, an urn or other decorative container can be transformed into a gently bubbling fountain.

A simple pool garden can be made out of a large watertight tub, like the half-barrels many garden centers and lumber yards sell for general planting use. It can be filled with water, planted with a dwarf water lily in a soil-filled basket in the center, and perhaps a few bog plants like irises or arrowheads around the sides and back, their pots propped up on bricks to just a few inches below water level.

For a larger and more permanent installation, ready-made pools are sold in many sizes and shapes in preformed fiberglass, and in flexible plastic pool liners that can be cut to fit, by firms that specialize in water-garden plants and supplies. For a floor-level pool, set a shell or liner into the ground during construction; an above-ground pool should be supported in a cushioning bed of sand or soil with sturdy sides made of landscaping timbers or concrete blocks. Or, you can dispense with the shell and build the pool out of reinforced, waterproofed concrete.

Ideally, a pool should have adjustable water inlet and a stoppered drain so that it can easily be filled, emptied, and cleaned. Adding underwater lights will dramatize the pool at night; and a string of three or four inexpensive, low-voltage fixtures can also be added around the pool and adjusted to highlight a changing arrangement of plants.

An above-ground pool has several advantages: it raises the water and plants so they are more visible, and the higher sides make it less likely that people, pets, dirt, and debris will accidentally fall in the water. The edges should be wide enough to display potted plants, and to sit on comfortably to tend the aquatic species or any ornamental fish in the pool.

To accommodate fish and a variety of water plants, including water lilies, the pool should be at least 18 inches deep; shallower ledges around the sides about 6 inches deep will support potted bog plants like water irises and pickerel weeds, which like only their roots in very damp soil. Finish the inside of the pool in dark gray or black, not swimming-pool blue: it will look far more like a natural pool, giving an impression of depth, heightening reflections, and setting off the plants to good effect.

Waterlilies and other flowering aquatic plants require maximum, high-intensity sun to bloom, at least four to six hours a day, though a few hybrids, like 'Daubeniana', will do reasonably well in less; they perform best in southerly latitudes where winter sun is relatively high and in areas where skies are generally clear.

Waterlilies, the stars of most water gardens, are available in many varieties and colors, ranging in size from pygmy types with flowers only an inch or so across to others with blooms as large as dinner plates. Hardy lilies native to temperate zones will grow in an indoor pool, but since

The his formal statuary pool is the focal point of a grand conservatory at Avery Hill near London. Dating from the early 19th century, aquatic plant houses shelter some of the most colorful and exotic tropical flowers from unfavorable northern climes.

they react to day length, most will go dormant in winter, as they do outdoors. More logical choices are the spectacular, fragrant tropical varieties, which in their native climates bloom virtually year-round. They have larger, more decorative leaves and flowers of every hue, including blues and purples, and bloom prolifically above the water on tall stems, not only displaying their blossoms but making them practical cut flowers. Mixing day-blooming tropical types, which close their flowers around dusk, and night-bloomers, which open about the same time, will produce a continuous display of color from midday to midnight.

Besides waterlilies, there are several smaller floating plants that are attractive in an indoor pool: water poppy (*Hydrocleys nymphoides*), which bears a profusion of small yellow blossoms; water lettuce (*Pistia stratiotes*), with free-floating roots and rosettes of pale blue-green leaves; and water snowflake (*Nymphoides cristatum*), which has small white flowers and lily-pad-like leaves.

If the scale of the garden room and pool warrant it, try a specimen or two of the stately lotus, with its large, upright leaves and fragrant flowers, or such tall, lacy foliage plants as the papyrus and umbrella palm.

To help keep the water clear, any pool will benefit from the addition of some submerged oxygenating plants—anarchis, eelgrass, cabomba, water milfoil, or parrot's-feather—

which compete with unsightly algae for nutrients and will also provide oxygen, food, and hiding places for ornamental fish.

Waterlilies, and other tropical species like lotus and papyrus, prefer warm night temperatures of 65 to 70 degrees and water temperatures in the same range, though established plants may tolerate 55 degrees. To raise water temperatures to the desired level without heating the whole greenhouse, you can use a small submersible electric heater, available from aquatic-plant or tropical fish suppliers.

IRIS
Iris

Many types of irises can be grown in shallow water or in well-watered pots around the edge of the pool, providing handsome, sword-shaped foliage and flowers ranging from white, yellow, and red to purple and blue. The crested iris, *I. cristata*, bears sweet-scented blue flowers on plants only about 6 inches high. Varieties of the Japanese iris, *I. kaempferi*, and the rabbit-ear iris, *I. laevigata*, grow about 2 feet tall and produce large, showy flowers in various hues. Of similar size is the yellow flag iris, *I. pseudacorus*, with bright yellow, brown-veined blossoms.

The sweet-scented crested iris, *Iris cristata*, is a charming miniature that grows only a few inches high. A native American woodland plant, it is not a true water plant but enjoys damp conditions and will thrive in containers placed near the edge of a garden pool.

LOTUS
Nelumbo

Smaller varieties of the tall, exotic, aromatic lotus are best suited to most indoor garden pools. A hybrid of *N. nucifera* named 'Momo Botan Minima' has 4- to 12-inch leaves and bears many-petalled, or "doubled", red flowers that rise 1 to 1½ feet out of the water. Another variety is the tulip lotus, *N. nucifera* 'Shirokunshi', which has tulip-shaped, creamy white flowers. For good bloom, lotuses should have full sun and water temperatures of 60 to 70 degrees or more.

PAPYRUS, UMBRELLA PALM
Cyperus

Dwarf papyrus, *C. haspans*, grows distinctive tufts of foliage atop stems 2 to 2½ feet high; the umbrella palm, *C. alternifolius*, bears whorls of palm-like leaves on stalks 3 to 5 feet tall. Both make fine accents arising from the water at the back of a pool.

WATER LILY
Nymphaea

Water lilies come in varieties to suit almost any taste. Smaller tropical day-bloomers, which produce great quantities of flowers about 4 inches across, include the white *N.* 'Marian Strawn', the yellow 'St. Louis', and the purple 'Panama Pacific'; the pink 'General Pershing' and 'Pink Perfection'; and the blue *N. colorata, N.* 'Daubeniana', 'Margaret Mary', and 'Mrs. Martin E. Randig'. Suitable night-blooming tropical lilies, which grow to a larger 6 inches indoors, include the rose-red 'Emily G. Hutchings' and the white 'Wood's White Knight'.

Among the hardy lilies appropriate for small indoor pools are such white hybrids as *N. tuberosa* and *N.* 'Marliacea Albida'; pinks like 'Marliacea Carnea'; yellows such as *N.* 'Marliacea Chromatella' and *N. pygmaea* 'Helvola' (the latter a true pygmy with flowers only 1 to 2 inches across); reds like 'Gloriosa' and 'James Brydon'; and "changeables" such as 'Graziella', whose blossoms begin as a light yellow with pink overtones and darken to reddish orange on successive days. Except for 'Helvola', all produce flowers about 3 to 4 inches across.

Water lilies need as much sun as possible. Hardy lilies will flower in water that is 65 degrees, but for good blooming, tropicals should have a water temperature of 70 degrees or more.

WATER POPPY
Hydrocleys

H. nymphoides has round, floating leaves up to 3 inches across that resemble small lily pads; its yellow, three-petaled flowers, about 2 inches in diameter, are held slightly above the water.

WATER SNOWFLAKE
Nymphoides

N. cristatum, which has leaves like miniature lily pads, produces an abun-

dance of tiny white flowers less than an inch across. Yellow snowflake, *N. geminata*, bears small, bright yellow blossoms above chocolate brown pads patterned with green veins.

WILD CALLA, WATER ARUM
Calla

Wild calla, *C. palustris*, is a good choice for planting at the shallow edge of a pool, sending up heart-shaped leaves on 8- to 12-inch stems and producing small white flowers that resemble miniature calla lilies.

Nymphaea, 'Panama Pacific', whose rich purple blossoms have glowing yellow centers, is one of several spectacular day-blooming tropical water lilies suitable for a garden-room pool.

Chapter Four

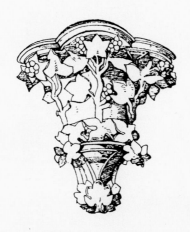

DESIGN DETAILS

In Victorian times, a conservatory was considered a "mark of elegance and refined enjoyment", as one observer put it, judged not only by its design and plantings but also by the sophisticated details that set it apart. In this modern French sunroom, tall windows suggest the same sort of elegance, while framing a splendid river view. An antique wicker chaise lounge adds an authentic 19th century touch.

A miniature garden under glass, this 19th century terrarium, set near a window to receive moderate light, provides a self-contained, naturally humid environment for small ferns and other moisture-loving plants. The glass top is hinged to allow access for planting, watering, pruning and, when needed, to admit fresh air.

Furniture designed for outdoor use is the most practical in a heavily planted garden room where humidity is often high. These metal chairs only hint at a classical style; other contemporary designs borrow heavily on their elaborately filigreed cast-iron Victorian predecessors, usually in lightweight cast aluminum.

For indoor shrubs and other larger plants, a classic choice is the so-called Versailles planter of white wood with a rigid waterproof liner, shown here from Foster-Kevil. Ornamental containers can be planted directly, or used as cache-pots to hide less glamorous pots.

A magnificently carved stone bench recalls designs traditionally used both indoors and out on private estates and in public parks. Like stone, wood furniture in hardwoods such as teak and mahogany ages beautifully.

Most well-designed indoor gardens have an ornamental focal point such as a large plant or an indoor pond. In the case of this Victorian conservatory, it is a small marble statue of a maiden, dramatically lighted among sculptured metal leaves and the lacy silhouettes of ferns.

The natural forms of flowers and sea shells adorning the base of a classical column are appropriate decorative motifs for the furnishings and accessories of a garden room.

Although sunlight is essential in a glass-enclosed space it must be controlled to avoid heat build-up and to protect sun-sensitive plants like ferns. Among the many shading devices available, this greenhouse uses exterior slatted blinds, which can reduce the light and heat levels by as much as half, and can be rolled up and out of the way in cool or cloudy weather when more light is desired.

Containers for plants come in great variety of shapes, sizes, and materials, from tiny, hand-painted porcelain bowls to large terra cotta tubs like the ones shown here, used for flowering tropical shrubs. Like their humbler cousin, the ordinary flowerpot, these porous clay containers allow excess water to evaporate and beneficial air to reach plant roots. Plastic containers are less likely to break and generally less expensive; being non-porous, they need less frequent watering but are easier to overwater. Newer plastic pots of the "self-watering" type avoid this problem by automatically feeding the right amount of moisture to the roots from built-in reservoirs.

The essence of the garden room is captured in a light-filled country solarium whose French doors open invitingly to the garden outside. The chair on which the gardener's hat awaits is a modern version of old-fashioned wicker, now enjoying a widespread revival. Made of woven split cane or rattan, it is both supple and light in weight, and comes in natural finishes, white or painted pastel colors.

Chapter Five

THE PRACTICALITIES

Construction and Equipment

A glass room, as luxurious as it may be, is often less expensive than a brick or wood home addition. Today, most garden rooms are built as conversions, or extensions, of existing spaces: a living room, kitchen, bedroom, bathroom or entry hall; often enclosing an open porch, patio, rooftop setback, or deck. Of prime importance in planning any garden room are its uses and location. A passive solar sunroom or working greenhouse, for example, will have more stringent light requirements than a dining room enlargement or bathroom renovation. A working greenhouse also needs good drainage and access to water and electricity.

Once you have a general idea of what sort of garden room you want, an architect, designer, or contractor specializing in solar or residential remodeling can help with the planning and design. Many architects are willing to work on an hourly fee basis, at least initially, to discuss possibilities and come up with ideas. Once your needs and the site restrictions have been considered, an architect will draw up a standard contract to complete preliminary and working drawings, help choose a contractor, and supervise construction. A good architect will not only tailor an addition to meet specific requirements, and do it imaginatively, but will also handle the often time-consuming and problematic negotiations with contractors and suppliers.

The most practical shape for a garden room is a rectangle, with its length along the side of the house measuring about one and a half to two times its projecting width. The greater the glass area facing south the more sun it will trap; and the greater the wall area the sunroom shares with the house, the greater the economy of construction and potential for a passive solar exchange of heat between the two.

For maxiumum sunlight throughout the day and year—the optimum condition for many plants, particularly flowering ones, and for a passive solar structure—a garden room should be located with a southern exposure. In the summer, sunlight will fall on the east and west sides of the site. But during the winter in northerly latitudes, the arc of the sun is so low that it strikes mainly the south side of a house. There are means to capture winter sun for rooms on the north, east, or west sides of a house, such as south-facing clerestory windows that project over a lower roof, and a professional may be able to suggest other solutions. Since the seasonal path of the sun varies slightly even between Boston and New York, any design should be tailored for the particular location.

For year-round morning sunlight, a southeasterly orientation is best, and is a good choice for a breakfast room. A southwest exposure yields more afternoon sun, while a garden room facing due west might provide a nice sunset view but will require more shading against hot afternoon rays, especially in summer. A north-facing garden room is suitable for an artists' studio or a greenhouse for plants that thrive in lower light intensities, as northern light is cool, shadowless, and indirect.

To convert a given area economically, it may be that the replacement of small windows with sliding glass doors, a window greenhouse, or the introduction of skylights will add sufficient natural light for both people and plants. Sliding glass doors can unify a patio or backyard with the house interior, while skylights provide illumination with privacy, particularly for second-floor or attic rooms, and window greenhouses benefit from the humidity and warmth of bathrooms and kitchens. These options are also practical when less imposing solutions are called for because the design of the house cannot be disturbed.

Standard Units

Whether your garden room is architect-designed or not, a prefabricated model might be adapted to suit your needs and tastes. These units, which are generally cheaper than a custom built design, come in a wide variety of sizes and shapes, from glorified bay windows 3 feet deep and 8 feet long to two-story solariums 20 feet deep and more than 50 feet long. Many prefabricated greenhouses are also flexible enough to be easily and inexpensively modified to specifications.

Quite a few prefabricated units are modular, and can be purchased in sections as required. As in any building project, a common tendency is to keep to a tight budget and order the minimum. This can be a false economy; frequently people discover that the new space is so popular it quickly seems too small. Installing a slightly larger model can actually yield as much as 50 percent more space at only 25 percent greater cost.

Smaller units can be erected by a reasonably ambitious homeowner over the course of a few summer weekends, with the instructions provided by the manufacturer, but it is wise to leave the foundations, structural alterations to the house, plumbing and wiring to professionals.

Manufacturers generally list prices for various models according to the size or number of sections desired. They also quote prices for various options: single, double, triple, tinted, and safety glass; straight or curving eaves; and added features such as operable windows, doors, vents, fans, plant benches, shading devices, and motorized, automatic controls.

Structure

Some prefabricated units have a structural framework of wooden members, which can be sealed with a clear preservative or covered with stain or paint to resist moisture and prolong its life. Wood transmits less heat and cold than metal, but the members are also heavier and thicker, both physically and visually, and they do block somewhat more of the sun's rays. While some people prefer the natural, substantial look of wood as an integral extension of a house, most greenhouse and solarium manufacturers today use aluminum, which is lighter, slimmer, corrosion-resistant, and requires virtually no maintenance. The framework is usually available in plain aluminum, dark bronze, or white baked-enamel finishes, though other colors may be specified. The best units have secure seals between structure and glazing to prevent air and water leakage; thermal gaskets or "breaks" to minimize conduction through the metal; and gutters to channel away any condensation on the inside of the glass so it does not drip annoyingly into the interior. If a greenhouse is improperly insulated from air and water, heating and cooling will be more difficult to control and more expensive. A few manufacturers, such as Pella, aim for the best of both worlds, employing the architectural appeal of wood exposed on the inside but clad on the outside with durable aluminum in a baked enamel finish of white or dark brown.

Glazing

The cheapest glazing of all is polyethylene film, stretched over a simple home-made framework to form an economical, temporary greenhouse for winter use. The plastic is removed when summer arrives, and so is really only suitable for winter plant protection. Polyethylene is flimsy and soon deteriorates, and thus is hardly suitable for a permanent garden room or greenhouse.

Rigid plastics like fiberglass and acrylic are far more durable, and resist breakage better, than ordinary glass, but most are translucent rather than transparent, and being softer are more easily scratched; they admit ample diffused light for plant growing and general enjoyment, but they do obscure the view. For these reasons rigid plastics are most commonly used in the ceiling sections of a garden room, where they can soften overhead summer sun and stand up to such hazards as hailstorms or falling branches. In these applications they can also take the place of overhead wire-reinforced safety glass, required by building regulations in many areas where a greenhouse-type structure is to be used as a living space.

Translucent rigid plastics can also be used on the end walls of a garden room to block undesirable views, or anywhere else a measure of privacy is desired (such as in a garden room that is also a bedroom or bathroom). Some acrylics come in ribbed panels with air spaces sandwiched between the inner and outer layers, providing greater insulating value and thus helping to lessen both condensation and heating costs.

Despite the advantages of certain plastics, glass is still the material of choice for most garden rooms. It is the most transparent, providing maximum daylight; it can be cleaned repeatedly without much danger of scratching, and unlike some plastics, it will not deteriorate or discolor with the passage of time.

Glass used in high-quality construction today is usually strong enough to resist breakage under normal conditions (generally it is ⅛-inch thick and referred to as "double strength"). Recommended by many greenhouse manufacturers, tempered glass is more expensive than ordinary annealed glass. But it is several times stronger, and in the event that it does break under a severe blow, it crumbles rather than shatters into harmless small pieces. Sliding glass doors are usually made of tempered glass, and many building codes require that it—or laminated glass of the type used in automobile windshields, with a plastic-film interlayer that prevents broken glass from falling out—be used in any overhead glazing as well. In a

garden room used by active children, or for parties, tempered glass may be a wise idea.

In a relatively mild climate, a single thickness of ⅛-inch glass may be the best, as well as the most economical, choice for a garden room, particularly one used to grow sun- and heat-loving plants. It transmits up to 90 percent of visible daylight, and the most solar heat.

If summer sun is especially strong, or if sky, sand, or nearby water produce considerable glare, some form of shading and/or glass with shading qualities is necessary. Bronze-tinted single glazing, offered by many manufacturers, reduces daylight transmission to around 70 percent or less, but cuts heat gain to 86 percent. Bronze-tinted reflecting glass, coated with a transparent oxide, reflects still more light, cutting transmission to 27 percent and heat gain to 54 percent. Such tinted or reflecting glass can be used just on the roof section against sky glare or overhead sun, or on the entire garden room. While it reduces the amount of natural daylight reaching the plants—and tints the light transmitted in a way some homeowners may find unappealing—in hot climates it can cut down considerably on heat gain and thus on air-conditioning bills.

For cooler climates, an insulating glass—which traps air between sealed layers to reduce heat transfer—may well repay its extra expense in savings on heating bills. Double glazing, the most familiar insulating glass,

reduces light transmission to a little over 80 percent and heat gain to 86 percent, but at the same time it cuts heat loss from inside to outside by more than half, so that on a winter night cumulative heat loss is half what it would be with single glazing. Triple glazing reduces light transmission to around 75 percent and heat gain to 82 percent, but it also cuts heat loss still more to about one-third that of ordinary single glazing.

Also coming into use is a new family of low-emissivity or "low-e" coatings on glass—thin layers of metal oxides that admit light and solar heat, then "trap" the heat inside by reflecting radiation. First introduced in the late 1970s, low-e is now being developed by several glass makers in more durable and easily handled coatings that are becoming increasingly popular. Low-e coatings are not only energy efficient, but have several other benefits: they make the inside glass warmer to the touch on a cold winter night, reduce condensation, and block much of the ultraviolet light that fades fabrics indoors.

Shading Devices

A problem with many garden rooms is that they receive not too little but too much sun; the high, hot sun of summer in particular can not only build up inside to temperatures distinctly uncomfortable for people but can also scorch and dry out plants. (Most plants do not enjoy temperatures over 85°F.)

The traditional solution, still used by some commercial greenhouse growers, is to paint the outside of the glass with a temporary shading compound resembling whitewash—a messy chore that eliminates the view from inside and hardly improves the structure's looks (the compound, in theory, is supposed to wear off gradually in the rain, but it often becomes blotchy, and at the end of the summer it may have to be scrubbed off).

Most garden rooms use some kind of permanent or movable shading device. The most effective are those placed outside the structure, where they intercept the rays before they penetrate inside and build up heat. Among the simplest is a deciduous tree or trees planted to the southwest, which will shade at least some of the room from the hottest summer sun, dropping its leaves in fall to admit the winter sun. However, a large tree, even when bare of leaves, can still block out much of the winter sun, so be careful about the trunk size and placement. Natural shading can also be provided by fast-growing annual vines, or deciduous perennial vines, trained to trellises placed around or over the structure.

Still greater control is provided by coverings placed directly over the glass. Woven plastic cloth, or lightweight plastic or aluminum slats, will provide anywhere from 50 to 75 percent shade while still admitting diffused natural light. These materials come in rolls that are attached to the top of the glass where it meets the house, and are operated by ropes and pulleys to provide the amount of shade required at any given time. A disadvantage is that they must be operated from outside (unless a motorized system that can be activated from inside is installed).

Shades can also be put up on the interior, where they are protected from the elements and more convenient to adjust. Lengths of shading cloth, muslin, or thin matchstick bamboo can simply be attached to the framework and stretched or loosely draped across the ceiling or down the walls wherever filtering of the sun is desired, such as a western exposure or over plants particularly sensitive to hot sun.

Horizontal or vertical louver blinds that operate in tracks are probably the most versatile shading as they can be pivoted to let in more or less light or drawn entirely out of the way; some have coatings specifically designed to reflect sun and radiated heat. Some manufacturers such as Pella build in narrow-slat horizontal blinds between the inner and outer layers of glass, to control movement of heat more efficiently and protect the blinds from damage and dirt.

Among the most sophisticated and expensive devices are "quilts" that shade by day and act as insulation at night by holding in accumulated warmth. Offered by some greenhouse manufacturers, these sandwich as many as five layers of insulated fabric, along with a vapor barrier, in a relatively thin blanket that is motor-operated on channels set in the greenhouse framework. The blanket can be moved to various settings and can be closed completely on cold winter nights but will proportionately block out light and view.

Some garden room designs solve the problem of overheating by eliminating overhead glass in favor of a solid, well-insulated roof, or extending the eaves several feet out from the house just far enough to block high summer rays yet allow lower winter sun to penetrate to warm the rear wall.

Ventilation

With or without shading, a garden room will require ventilation. Plants as well as people need fresh air, and both suffer in a stagnant or overly humid atmosphere, particularly when temperatures pass 80 degrees.

In a relatively moderate climate, adequate ventilation may be provided simply by locating doors, windows, or operable glass jalousie louvers (equipped with insect screens, if necessary) so that prevailing summer breezes sweep in one side of the room and out the other. Equally, operable vents low on the outside wall—hinged glass panels that open outward like awnings to keep rain from getting inside—and similar ones at the ridge, will draw in cool air below and allow hot air to rise out through the roof. Such vents can be operated manually, but are most practical when connected to an electric motor and thermostat, which will open or close them automatically when a preset temperature is reached.

Some kind of fan is almost essential in a garden room unless it has very good cross-ventilation. A slowly rotating ceiling or "paddle" fan will mix stratified layers of different temperatures, cooling occupants below and washing plants with a gentle, constant movement of air. (On a cold winter day, the fan will also bring warm air down from the ceiling.)

A greenhouse exhaust fan high on one end wall, with a set of intake louvers on the opposite wall, will also vent hot air and bring in cooler outside air. For optimum performance, the exhaust fan should face away from, not into, prevailing winds, and its opening should be sealed from the elements by outward-pivoting louvers that open automatically when the fan is on. On the opposite wall, the fresh-air intake louvers should pivot inward and be powered by a small electric motor. The whole system should be wired to a thermostat that turns it on automatically when the temperature reaches a preset level, such as 80 or 85 degrees. To keep the temperatures at a level suitable for people and plants, the thermostat should be placed at shoulder or waist level, shaded from direct sun.

Further refinements are possible if the garden room is a separate space, divided from the main part of the house by sliding doors or by the original exterior wall. Rather than waste sun-heated air in winter by venting it outside, it can be vented directly into the house, either by opening windows or doors or by cutting small openings into the house wall just below the ridge (which can be ducted to warm upstairs rooms). A reversible, thermostatically controlled fan in the rear wall of a garden room will pump warm air into the house even more effectively. This same fan can also be used to pump warm air from the house into the garden room at night, helping to maintain safe temperatures for plants during cold weather. (To avoid annoying noise, any fan in a garden room should be of a belt-driven or other quiet-running type.)

Garden rooms in warm areas, particularly those used primarily as plant greenhouses, can benefit from evaporative cooling units. Such units will lower inside temperatures by as much as 20 to 30 degrees, using fans to draw warm outside air through filters that are kept moist, lowering its temperature by evaporation, and discharging the cooled, moistened air into the room. Any garden room, of course, can be air conditioned, either separately or as part of the house, but make sure temperature and humidity are maintained at levels acceptable to plants as well as people.

The Solar Garden Room

A well-designed garden room can heat itself, and lower energy bills for the rest of the house, but it is here that the somewhat muddled distinction between a greenhouse and a sunroom or solarium should be borne clearly in mind.

A true greenhouse uses as much glass as possible, on all available sides, to receive uniform, evenly distributed sunlight for plants; if extra heating is necessary to counter heat loss on cold winter days, that's an acceptable cost of enjoying the plants one likes to grow.

A sunroom, particularly a cold-climate one that is expected to contribute free heat to the house, has to be designed with additional criteria in mind. For maximum solar gain, a southern exposure is mandatory. The angle of the glass should ideally be such that the sun's rays hit it perpendicularly, so that most of them penetrate the interior instead of bouncing off obliquely (at the latitude of Boston, for example, the ideal angle is 52 to 57 degrees from horizontal).

In a sunroom designed for solar heating, the all-glass end walls of a greenhouse may be more of a thermal liability than an asset in gaining sunlight. A window or glass door in the east-facing end will let in some welcome morning sun, helping to warm the room after a cold night. But a more solid, heavily insulated wall on the west may be preferable to minimize heat loss, and reduce overheating in summer from hot western sun. A solid, projecting roof section, also heavily insulated, will further prevent heat loss while blocking unwanted high summer sun, and a solid "knee wall" a few feet high can further enclose the structure on the front, though it will reduce sunlit space for plants on the floor.

An efficiently-designed sunroom will absorb and store excess solar heat, and release it at night and during cloudy days. To do this, the room must have what solar designers call "thermal mass"—some heat retaining material. This can be provided by masonry: a floor of brick, quarry tile, flagstone, or crushed rock, and/or a back wall of stone, concrete block, or brick. The thicker the masonry the more heat it will store. Just as it helps to balance out low temperatures, thermal mass has a complementary advantage: by absorbing heat, it also helps to keep a garden room from overheating too quickly on hot summer days.

For still greater storage capacity, the best commonly available material is water, which, pound for pound, stores about four times as much heat energy as masonry. A rule of thumb often used in regions of the country that have moderate to cool climates is to provide a thermal mass of 2 to 3 gallons of water, or ½ to 1 cubic foot of masonry, per square foot of glazing in the room.

Water can be held in almost any kind of container. Ordinary plastic 1-gallon milk jugs or 5-gallon black metal paint cans lined up in rows and concealed under plant benches at the front of the room will get plenty of sun. Standard 55-gallon oil drums, painted black for easier heat absorp-

tion and set along the back of the room, perhaps partially disguised by a broad plant shelf laid on top, will hold a great deal of heat.

Greenhouse and solar equipment suppliers offer specially made, clear or translucent plastic cylinders, of various diameters and up to 8 feet high or more; shorter ones can be used in front, taller ones as far to the rear of the room as the winter sun will reach. When filling clear containers with water, it is wise to add an algicide to prevent the water turning a murky green. A dark blue dye added to the water will help it warm more quickly.

For those with limited space, or a scientific turn of mind, there are advanced, high-capacity thermal storage systems that make use of tubes, rods, or panels containing "phase change" compounds or eutectic salts. These chemicals melt at high daytime temperatures, absorbing large quantities of heat, then return to their solid state as the temperature drops, releasing the heat to the room.

A separate, tightly built sunroom can be thermally self-sufficient, if night temperatures of 45 or 50 degrees are acceptable, and it can actually cut the heating bills for the rest of the house by as much as half. If the temperature drops below this level, a sliding door or window opened slightly will let some house heat into the room, or a portable electric heater can be placed on the floor near especially cold-sensitive plants.

To keep a garden room at more

comfortable temperatures for people, or higher ones for tropical plants, the house heating system can be extended to serve it or a space heater installed as a backup during cold days or nights.

Floors, Walls, and Ceilings

The flooring in any sunroom subject to constant use should of course be long-wearing, moisture-proof, and easy to keep clean, particularly if plants are set on the floor, where dampness can accumulate under their pots and ruin carpets or wood. A good all-round choice is ceramic tile, made of a mixture of clays fired at high temperatures. Ceramic tile is available in sizes from 4 to 24 inches across (most commonly 6 to 8 inches), and in square, rectangular, hexagonal, and fancy-edged shapes. One type is terra cotta, the classic, brick-colored material that has been used in garden settings indoors and out since ancient times. Others include vitrified stoneware and so-called quarry tile, which come in a range of warm, earthy browns, reds, and yellows. Tiles with glazed surfaces look nice and shiny, but they can be slippery when wet; unglazed tiles are preferable because they have greater skid resistance—some incorporate textures and/or an abrasive to provide even greater friction—and at the same time are easily cleaned with a damp mop.

For maximum water resistance, tiles should be set in, and the joints grouted with, a latex portland cement. Their surface needs no waxing or other finishing, although terra cotta is sometimes treated with a sealer made of one part boiled linseed oil to two parts mineral-spirit paint thinner, allowed to dry for 24 hours or more, and then waxed. A floor of ceramic tile, laid on a concrete slab, makes a good passive solar collector; darker colors in particular readily absorb sun warmth during the day and gradually release it at night to keep temperatures from falling too low.

If small children play on the floor, it will be easier on their knees and elbows if at least part of a tile area is covered with carpeting, or with a soft throw rug that is backed by a skid-resistant rubber mat. An alternative is to cover the entire room with a more resilient, and usually less expensive, plastic flooring. Vinyl tile comes in 9-by 9-inch and 12-by 12-inch sizes and is relatively easy to lay; vinyl sheet flooring, which comes in rolls 6 or 12 feet wide, is a bit harder to install but makes a virtually seamless, waterproof floor. Vinyl flooring comes in almost all designs and colors imaginable, including ones with shiny "no-wax" surfaces and decorative patterns.

Areas away from plants or heavy traffic can be carpeted. Good choices include open-weave "straw" matting (actually made of sisal hemp or coir), which has a natural, summery look and dries relatively quickly if water is spilled on it. Pile carpets provide a wider range of colors and patterns, but ones made of wool, nylon, or polyester may eventually fade in the bright sun. Better choices are acrylic, which has a naturally long color life, and polypropylene, which is usually treated to resist fading; they are also less expensive and resist mildew and soiling.

Wall and ceiling finishes should also be long-wearing and moisture-resistant. Least expensive, and easiest to apply, is a good grade of latex paint; choose an acrylic or enamel type that is washable, stain resistant, and colorfast. If you prefer wallpaper, use a vinyl-coated type that will wipe clean. Wood paneling lends a warm or rustic look, but it is wise to treat wood with a clear sealer and to avoid rough textures that collect grime.

Other Equipment

If you intend to do much gardening or entertaining in your garden room, its design should allow for easy access to water. A sink can be used for cleanup, and an adjoining countertop, with storage beneath for tools and supplies, will serve for anything from repotting plants to mixing drinks.

To water a number of plants or to wash down the floor occasionally to clean up dirt and raise humidity use small-caliber hose made for indoor watering, or the type of flat hose that rolls up neatly on a reel. In the crowded conditions of a plant-filled garden room, a long "watering wand" with a soft-spray nozzle on the end is almost invaluable for hanging bas-kets and other hard-to-reach plants.

Greenhouse suppliers and garden centers also offer various kinds of automatic watering systems, including drip irrigation tubes and capillary watering mats. But because pebble trays and a good soil medium can usually hold enough water for a day or two, automatic watering systems are usually most cost-efficient for those gardeners who must be away from their plants for days at a time.

For advanced gardeners there are humidifiers to raise the moisture level in a room for plants that need it, and humidistats to turn the humidifiers on and off, as well as misters and automatic misting controls. A simple thermometer is a must for a garden room, but better still is a maximum-minimum thermometer that records high and low temperatures.

Among the other gadgets aimed at easing the indoor gardener's life, electric soil-heating cables, with or without thermostatic controls, are especially useful. Laid in the bottom of one or more plant benches, growing trays, or flats, they get seedlings off to a healthier start and promote sturdy root growth and general vigor among older plants. Better still, this added warmth in the soil means that air temperatures can be kept as much as 20 degrees lower than plants would otherwise demand, not only saving energy but also allowing you to grow more tropical species and encouraging some to flower year round.

Finally, if all the thermostats, automatic vents, and heating systems should somehow fail—either through a general power failure or their own darn fault—there is one gadget of last resort. It is a battery-powered greenhouse alarm that goes off whenever the temperature soars or plunges to dangerous levels, shrilly summoning the gardener to the rescue of his or her precious plants.

Sources of Supply

Following is a selection of firms and organizations that provide products and/or information for garden rooms. Most will send brochures, catalogues, or other literature on request.

Manufacturers of garden room and skylight units

Allstate Greenhouse Manufacturing Co.
1691 North Highway
Southampton, NY 11968
Cedar-framed units

Aluminum Greenhouses, Inc.
14605 Lorain Avenue
P.O. Box 11087
Cleveland, OH 44111
Freestanding and lean-to models

Andersen Corporation
Bayport, MN 55003
Windows, sliding glass doors, skylights

Archway Greenhouses
Box 246
Duck Hill, MS 38925
Freestanding hobby greenhouses

Brady and Sun
97 Webster Street
Worcester, MA 01603
Solar-heated sun space units

Four Seasons Greenhouses
425 Smith Street
Farmingdale, NY 11735
Various models with aluminum framing and single-, double-, or triple-glazing

Gardener's Supply Co.
128 Intervale Road
Dept. PH073
Burlington, VT 05401
Small freestanding greenhouses for northern climates

Garden Way Inc.
430 Hudson River Road
Waterford, NY 12188
Solar-heated sunroom and greenhouse units

Greenhouses by Bromack
6554 East 41st Street
Tulsa, OK 74145
Aluminum and glass greenhouses

Habitat
123 Elm Street
South Deerfield, MA 01373
Double-glazed units with aluminum-clad wooden frames and insulated cedar roofs

Hurd Millwork Company
520 South Whelen Avenue
Medford, WI 54451
Aluminum-clad wood windows and patio doors

Janco Greenhouses
9390 Davis Avenue
Laurel, MD 20707
Wide variety of aluminum-framed sunrooms and greenhouse units

Lord & Burnham
2 Main Street
Irvington, NY 10533
Wide variety of aluminum-framed sunrooms and greenhouse units

Machin Designs (U.S.A.) Inc.
P.O. Box 167
Rowayton, CT 06853
Modern sunrooms and conservatories inspired by Victorian models

Mellinger's Inc.
2310 West South Range Road
North Lima, OH 44452
Inexpensive greenhouse units

National Greenhouse Company
P.O. Box 100
Pana, IL 62557
Attached and freestanding greenhouses and sunrooms

Naturalite, Inc.
3233 West Kingsley Road
Garland, TX 75041
Custom and prefabricated skylights

Northern Sun
P.O. Box 957
Lynnwood, WA 98046
Solar units with cedar frames and insulating glass

Pella/Rolscreen Company
100 Main Street
Pella, IA 50219
Modular sunrooms, skylights, entry units,
sliding glass doors

Princeton Energy Group
575 Ewing Street
Princeton, NJ 08540
Custom sun spaces

Roto Frank of America, Inc.
Research Park, P.O. Box 599
Chester, CT 06412
Skylights

Rough Brothers, Inc.
P.O. Box 16010
Cincinnati, OH 45216
Aluminum and glass greenhouses

Santa Barbara Greenhouses
390 Dawson Drive
Camarillo, CA 93010
Fiberglass units

Solar Resources, Inc.
P.O. Box 1848
Taos, NM 87571
Greenhouses and solar rooms

Sturdi-Built Manufacturing Co.
11304 S.W. Boones Ferry Road
Portland, OR 97219
Redwood-framed greenhouses

Sun Systems Solar Greenhouses
60 Vanderbilt Motor Parkway
Commack, NY 11725
Aluminum-framed, double-glazed models

Sunglo Solar Greenhouses
4441 26th Avenue West
Seattle, WA 98199
Attached and freestanding models

Suntech Inc.
168 Montowese Street
Branford, CT 06405
Aluminum and redwood freestanding,
lean-to, and window units

Texas Greenhouse Co.
2713 St. Louis Avenue
Fort Worth, TX 76110
Aluminum and redwood freestanding,
lean-to, and window units

Turner Greenhouses
Box 1260
Goldsboro, NC 27530
Prefabricated greenhouses

Vegetable Factory, Inc.
71 Vanderbilt Avenue
New York, NY 10017
Solar greenhouses

Velux-America Inc.
155 West Street
Wilmington, MA 01887
Skylight units

Ventarama Skylight Corp.
Hicksville, NY 11801
Skylight units

Wasco Products, Inc.
P.O. Box 351
Sanford, ME 04073
Skylight units

Manufacturers—England

Alitex Greenhouses
19 St. John's Works
Station Road
Alton
Hampshire GU34 2PZ, England
Lean-to and freestanding greenhouses

Amdega Ltd.
Faverdale
Darlington
Durham DL3 OPW, England
Modular cedar-framed conservatories

Baco Leisure Products, Ltd.
Windover Road
Huntingdon PE 18 7EH, England
Freestanding and attached aluminum
greenhouses

Banbury Homes & Gardens, Ltd.
P.O. Box 17
Banbury
Oxfordshire, OX17 3NS, England
Cedar-framed greenhouses

Alexander Bartholomew
79 Ravenscourt Road
London W6, England
Modular conservatories framed in red pine
and mahogany

Cambridge Greenhouse Co., Ltd.
Comberton
Cambridge CB3 7BY, England
Freestanding aluminum greenhouses

Clear Span Ltd.
Greenfield
Oldham
Lancashire PH3 7AG, England
Freestanding and attached aluminum greenhouses

Machin Designs, Inc.
Ransome's Dock
Park Gate Road
London SW11 4NP, England
(see Machin Designs, U S A)

Maston & Langinger Ltd.
Hall Staithe
Fakenham
Norfolk MR21 9BW, England
Custom and prefabricated conservatories

C.H. Whitehouse Ltd.
Buckhurst Works
Frant
Sussex, England
Freestanding cedar-framed greenhouses

Sources of Plants

Popular ornamental, vegetable, and fruit plants can be obtained at local garden centers, florists, and nurseries; vegetable and flower seeds through mail-order seed companies. Following are some of the firms that specialize in a wider range of varieties, including hard-to-find ones.

Alberts & Merkel Bros.
2210 South Federal Highway
Boynton Beach, FL 33435
Tropical plants

The Banana Tree
715 Northampton Street
Easton, PA 18042
Tropical plants

W. Atlee Burpee Co.
300 Park Avenue
Warminster, PA 18991
Flower and vegetable seeds; perennials, shrubs, fruits

Greenland Flower Shop
R.D. 1
Port Matilda, PA 16870
Houseplants

Gurney's Seed & Nursery Co.
Yankton, SD 57079
Vegetable and flower seeds; houseplants, fruits, shrubs

International Growers Exchange
P.O. Box 52248
Livonia, MI 48152
Houseplants

Harris Seeds
Moreton Farm
3670 Buffalo Road
Rochester, NY 14624
Vegetable and flower seeds

J & L Orchids
20 Sherwood Road
Easton, CT 06812
Miniature orchids

Jones & Scully, Inc.
18955 S.W. 168th Street
Miami, FL 33187
Many varieties of orchids

Kartuz Greenhouses
1408 Sunset Drive
Vista, CA 92083
Houseplants

Lauray of Salisbury
Undermountain Road
Salisbury, CT 06068
Houseplants

Lilypons Water Gardens
Lilypons, MD 21717
Waterlilies, other aquatic plants

Logee's Greenhouses
55 North Street
Danielson, CT 06239
Begonias, geraniums, rare houseplants

Merry Gardens
P.O. Box 595
Camden, ME 04843
Houseplants

Nor'East Miniature Roses, Inc.
58 Hammond Street
Rowley, MA 01969
Miniature roses

George W. Park Seed Co.
Greenwood, SC 29647
Vegetable, flower and houseplant seeds, and bulbs

Shady Hill Gardens
821 Walnut Street
Batavia, IL 60510
Many varieties of geraniums

Shepherd's Garden Seeds
7389 West Zayante Road
Felton, CA 95018
European vegetable seeds

Terrestris Greenhouses
409 East 60th Street
New York, NY 10022
Indoor plants

Thompson & Morgan, Inc.
P.O. Box 1308
Jackson, NJ 08527
Flower, vegetable, houseplant seeds

Van Bourgondien Bros.
P.O. Box A
245 Farmingdale Rd.
Rt. 109
Babylon, NY 11702
Houseplants, perennials, bulbs

Wayside Gardens
Hodges, SC 29695
Houseplants, perennials, bulbs

White Flower Farm
Litchfield, CT 06759
Perennials, bulbs, houseplants

Sources of Plant Information

African Violet Society of America, Inc.
P.O. Box 3609
Beaumont, TX 77704

American Begonia Society, Inc.
P.O. Box 1129
Encinitas, CA 92024

American Fuchsia Society
Hall of Flowers
Golden Gate Park
San Francisco, CA 94122

American Gloxinia and Gesneriad
Society, Inc.
P.O. Box 493
Beverly Farms, MA 01915

American Hibiscus Society
P.O. Drawer 5430
Pompano Beach, FL 33064

American Iris Society
7414 East 60th Street
Tulsa, OK 74145

American Orchid Society, Inc.
6000 South Olive Avenue
West Palm Beach, FL 33405

American Rock Garden Society
c/o Norman Singer
Norfolk Road
South Sandisfield, MA 01255

American Rose Society
P.O. Box 3000
Shreveport, LA 71130

Bromeliad Society, Inc.
c/o Linda Harbert
2488 East 49th
Tulsa, OK 74105

Cactus and Succulent Society of
America, Inc.
c/o Virginia Martin
2631 Fairgreen Avenue
Arcadia, CA 91006

Cymbidium Society of America, Inc.
c/o Mrs. Richard L. Johnston
6881 Wheeler Avenue
Westminster, CA 92683

Epiphyllum Society of America
Box 1395
Monrovia, CA 91016

Garden Club of America
598 Madison Avenue
New York, NY 10022

Gardenia Society of America
Box 879
Atwater, CA 95301

Gesneriad Society International
P.O. Box 549
Knoxville, TN 37901

Hoya Society International
P.O. Box 54271
Atlanta, GA 30308

Indoor Citrus and Rare Fruit Society
176 Coronado Avenue
Los Altos, CA 94022

Indoor Gardening Society of America, Inc.
c/o Horticultural Society of New York
128 West 58th Street
New York, NY 10019

International Geranium Society
5861 Walnut Drive
Eureka, CA 95581

International Palm Society
Box 27
Forestville, CA 95436

International Tropical Fern Society
8720 S.W. 34th Street
Miami, FL 33165

Los Angeles International Fern Society
c/o Don Woods
9914 Calmada Avenue
Whittier, CA 90605

National Fuchsia Society
c/o George Ghiotto
702 Sunrise Boulevard
Long Beach, CA 90806

Saintpaulia International
The Meadows, Condo 1075
7914 Gleason Road
Knoxville, TN 37919

Terrarium Association
57 Wolfpit Road
Norwalk, CT 06851

Garden Room and Greenhouse Accessories

American Beauty Products
117 25th Street South
Irondale, AL 35210
Garden furniture

Architectural Fiberglass
1330 Bellevue Street
P.O. Box 8100
Green Bay, WI 54308
Contemporary indoor-outdoor furniture and fiberglass plant containers

Barrington Industries
P.O. Box 133
Barrington, IL 60010
Wide range of greenhouse equipment and supplies

Bench Manufacturing Co
P.O. Box 66
Essex Street Station
Boston, MA 02112
Wood benches, planters, picnic tables

Brown-Jordan
9860 Gidley Street
Box 5688
El Monte, CA 91734
Contemporary garden furniture

Cat's Cradle, Ltd.
3585 Lawson Boulevard
Oceanside, NY 11572
Hand-screened canvas hammocks

Christopher Design
1901 South Great S.W. Parkway
Suite 214
Grand Prairie, TX 75051
Bent willow indoor-outdoor furniture

Clapper's
1125 Washington Street
West Newton, MA 02165
*Wide range of garden accessories and
equipment; mail-order catalogue*

Country Casual
17317 Germantown Road
Germantown, MD 20874
English-style teak garden furniture

Designplace Furniture Manufacturing Co.
1326 Hill Street
El Cajon, CA 92020
Redwood and metal garden furniture

Foster-Kevill
15102 Weststate Street
Westminster, CA 92683
Traditional wood planters

The Garden Concepts Collection
P.O. Box 241233
Memphis, TN 38124
Garden furniture and accessories

Gardener's Eden
P.O. Box 7307
San Francisco, CA 94120
*Wide range of garden accessories,
equipment, and furniture; mail order
catalogue*

Gro-Tek Home Greenhouse Supplies
RFD 1
South Berwick, ME 03908
Greenhouse supplies

Imagineering, Inc.
P.O. Box 97
Rockport, ME 04856
Ready-made and custom garden furniture

Indoor Gardening Supplies
Box 40567
Detroit, MI 48240
Greenhouse supplies

Moultrie Manufacturing Co.
P.O. Drawer 1179
Moultrie, GA 31768
*Aluminum replicas of Victorian cast-iron
garden furniture; planters, fountains,
and urns*

Skagit Gardens
1695 Johnson Road
Mount Vernon, WA 98273
Greenhouse supplies

Smith & Hawken
25 Corte Madera
Mill Valley, CA 94941
*Wide range of garden accessories,
equipment, and furniture; mail-order
catalogue*

Speake Garden Furnishings
351 Peachtree Hills Avenue N.E. #505B
Atlanta, GA 30305
Reproductions of English garden furniture

Tennessee Fabricating Co.
2366 Prospect Street
Memphis, TN 38106
*Reproductions of Victorian garden
furniture in cast-iron and aluminum*

White Swan, Ltd.
8104 S.W. Nimbus Avenue
Beaverton, OR 97005
Teak benches and garden accessories

The Wicker Garden
1318 Madison Avenue
New York, NY 10028
Wicker furniture

WickerWorks
267 Eighth Street
San Francisco, CA 94103
Wicker furniture

Zona
97 Greene Street
New York, NY 10013
Garden furniture and accessories

INDEX

ACKNOWLEDGMENTS

The author is especially grateful to Viki Ferreniea, Horticulturist of the New Canaan, Connecticut, Nature Center, for her expert assistance, and for the help of Charles B. Thomas and Rolf Nelson of Lilypons Water Gardens, Lilypons, Maryland, and Patrick Nutt of Pennsylvania's Longwood Gardens.

Smallwood & Stewart would like to thank Nora Humphrey and Anne-Marie Ehrlich for picture research; Sally Smallwood and Jean Coombes for their help in finding locations; Stephen Morse and Robert Graf; Leslie Fagan and Liz Saft.

PICTURE CREDITS

8, Jerry Harpur
14, Lynne Bryant/
Arcaid
15, Lynne Bryant/
Arcaid
16, Dick Sims
17, Dick Sims
18, Derek Fell
19, Derek Fell
20, Pamla Toler
21, Pamla Toler
22, Pamla Toler
23, Pamla Toler
24, Gilles de Chabaneix
26, Pamla Toler
27, Pamla Toler
28, Carol Sharp
29, Carol Sharp
30, Derry Moore
31, Derry Moore
32, Hugh Olliff
33, Maison de Marie
Claire/J.C. Pratt/
Belmont
34, Maison de Marie
Claire/J.C.Pratt/
D.Pries
35, Lord & Burnham
36, Maison de Marie
Claire/Rozes/
Hirsch

37, Derek Fell
38, Maison de Marie
Claire/J.C.Pratt/
D.Pries
39, Maison de Marie
Claire/J.C.Pratt/
D.Pries
40, Karen Halverson
41, Karen Halverson
42, Ezra Stoller/
ESTO
42, Stephen Tilly
43, Norman McGrath
44, Maison de Marie
Claire/Hussenot/
Belmont
46, Norman McGrath
47, Tim Street-Porter
48, Karen Bussolini
49, Karen Bussolini
50, Clive Frost
51, Ianthe Ruthven
52, Ron Sutherland
53, Ron Sutherland
54, Angela Coombes
55, Elizabeth Whiting
& Assocs.
56, Joshua Greene
57, Joshua Greene
58, Tim Street-Porter

59, Maison de Marie
Claire/Hussenot/
Belmont
60, McGregor Lanier
Assoc.
61, Robert Perron
62, Tim Street-Porter
63, Tim Street-Porter
66, Victor Watts
67, Maison de Marie
Claire/J.C.Pratt/
D.Pries
67, Michael Datoli
68, Jessie Walker
70, Ezra Stoller/
ESTO
70, Maison de Marie
Claire/J.C.Pratt/
D.Pries
71, Tim Street-Porter
72, Elizabeth Whiting
& Assocs.
73, Maison de Marie
Claire/Hussenot/
Belmont
74, Maison de Marie
Claire/J.C.Pratt/
D.Pries
75, Ianthe Ruthven
76, Ianthe Ruthven
77, Ianthe Ruthven

78, Robert Harding
Picture Library
78, Pamla Toler
79, Ianthe Ruthven
80, Elizabeth Whiting
& Assocs.
81, Ezra Stoller/
ESTO
82, Lilo Raymond
83, Gary Mottau
83, Elizabeth Whiting
& Assocs
84, Gilles de
Chabaneix
85, Karen Bussolini
86, Jessie Walker
86, Lord & Burnham
87, Ezra Stoller/
ESTO
88, Maison de Marie
Claire/Bouchet/
Hourdin
89, Elizabeth Whiting
& Assocs.
91, Robert Perron
92, Ianthe Ruthven
93, Ron Sutherland
94, Karen Halverson
95, Ogden Tanner
96, Ron Sutherland
97, Ron Sutherland

98, Carolyn Bates
99, Ken Druse
99, John Glover
100, Lord & Burnham
101, Carolyn Bates
104, Derek Fell
105, Derry Moore
106, Clive Frost
107, Clive Frost
108, Jerry Harpur
109, Derek Fell
111, Dick Keen
112, Dick Keen
113, Derek Fell
114, Dick Keen
115, Dick Keen
115, Richard Brown
116, Derek Fell
117, Jerry Harpur
119, Dick Keen
120, Dick Keen
122, Pamla Toler
123, Pamela Harper
124, Derek Fell
126, Pamla Toler
127, Dick Keen
129, Dick Keen
130, Dick Keen
132, Pamela Harper
135, Pamela Harper
136, Pamela Harper

139, Janco Greenhouses
141, Clive Frost
142, Ogden Tanner
143, Lilypons Water
Gardens
146, Gilles de Chabaneix
147, David Stone
147, Dick Sims
148, Foster-Kevil
149, Pamla Toler
150, Pamla Toler
151, Pamla Toler
151, Felice Frankel
152, David Stone
153, Elizabeth Whiting
& Assocs.
176, Pamla Toler